THE
PHOENIX LIBRARY

*

SINCE CÉZANNE

SINCE CÉZANNE

By

CLIVE BELL

CHATTO AND WINDUS
LONDON

First published March 1922
Fourth printing January 1928
First issued in the Phoenix Library
1929

ACKNOWLEDGMENT

Most of these Essays appeared in THE NEW RE-
PUBLIC and THE ATHENAEUM : some, however,
are reprinted from THE BURLINGTON MAGAZINE,
THE NEW STATESMAN, and ART AND DECORA-
TION.   I take this opportunity of thanking the
editors of all.

C. B.

CONTENTS

SINCE CÉZANNE

With anyone who concludes that this preliminary essay is merely to justify the rather
appetizing title of my book I shall be at
no pains to quarrel. If privately I think it
does more, publicly I shall not avow it.
Historically and critically, I admit, the thing
is as slight as a sketch contained in five-
and-thirty pages must be, and certainly it
adds nothing to what I have said, in the
essays to which it stands preface, on æsthetic
theory. The function it is meant to perform
—no very considerable one perhaps—is to
justify not so much the title as the shape of
my book, giving, in the process, a rough
sketch of the period with certain aspects of
which I am to deal. That the shape needs
justification is attributable to the fact that
though all, or nearly all, the component articles
were written with a view to making one volume,
I was conscious, while I wrote them, of dealing
with two subjects. Sometimes I was discussing
current ideas, and questions arising out of a
theory of art ; at others I was trying to give
some account of the leading painters of the
contemporary movement. Sometimes I was
writing of Theory, sometimes of Practice.
By means of this preface I hope to show why,
at the moment, these two, far from being
distinct, are inseparable.

To understand thoroughly the contemporary

movement—that movement in every turn and twist of which the influence of Cézanne is traceable—the movement which may be said to have come into existence contemporaneously almost with the century, and still holds the field—it is necessary to know something of the æsthetic theories which agitated it. One of the many unpremeditated effects of Cézanne's life and work was to set artists thinking, and even arguing. His practice challenged so sharply all current notions of what painting should be that a new generation, taking him for master, found itself often, much to its dismay, obliged to ask and answer such questions as " What am I doing ? " " Why am I doing it ? " Now such questions lead inevitably to an immense query—" What is Art ? " The painters began talking, and from words sprang deeds. Thus it comes about that in the sixteen or seventeen years which have elapsed since the influence of Cézanne became paramount theory has played a part which no critic or historian can overlook. It is because to-day that part appears to be dwindling, because the influence of theory is growing less, that the moment is perhaps not inopportune for a little book such as this is meant to be. It comes, if I am right, just when the movement is passing out of its first into the second phase.

During this first phase theory has been much to the fore. But it has been theory, you must remember, working on a generation of direct and intensely personal artists. In so curious an alliance you will expect to find as much stress as harmony; also, you must remember, its headquarters were at Paris where flourishes the strongest and most vital tradition of painting extant. In this great tradition some of the more personal artists, struggling against the intolerable exactions of doctrine, have found powerful support ; indeed, only with its aid have they succeeded at last in securing their positions as masters who, though not disdaining to pay homage for what they hold from the new theories, are as independent as feudal princes. But the more I consider the period the more this strange and restless alliance of doctrine with temperament appears to be of its essence ; wherefore, I shall not hesitate to make of it a light wherewith to take a hasty look about me. Here are two labels ready to hand—" temperamental " and " doctrinaire." I am under no illusion as to the inadequacy and fallibility of both ; neither shall I imagine that, once applied, they are bound to stick. On the contrary, you will see, in a later chapter, how, having dubbed Matisse "temperamental" and Picasso "theorist," I come, on examination, to find in the art of Matisse so much science and in that of Picasso such extraordinary sensibility that in the end I am much inclined to pull off the labels and change them about. But, though for purposes of criticism coarse and sometimes treacherous, this pair of opposites—which are really quite compatible—may prove two useful hacks. As such I accept them; and by them borne along I now propose to make a short tour of inspection, one object of which will be to indicate broadly the lie of the land, another to call attention to a number of interesting artists whose names happen not to have come my way in any other part of this book.

I said, and I suppose no one will deny it, that Paris was the centre of the movement: from Paris, therefore, I set out. There the movement originated, there it thrives and develops, and there it can best be seen and understood. Ever since the end of the seventeenth century France has taken the lead in the visual arts, and ever since the early part of the nineteenth Paris has been the artistic capital of Europe. Thither painters of all foreign nations have looked ; there many have worked, and many more have made a point of showing their works. Any-one, therefore, who makes a habit of visiting Paris, seeing the big exhibitions, and frequenting dealers and studios, can get a pretty complete idea of what is going on in Europe. There he will find Picasso—the animator * of

* For this word, which I think very happily suggests Picasso's rôle in contemporary painting, I am indebted to my friend M. André Salmon.

4

the movement—and some of the best of his compatriots, Juan Gris and Marie Blanchard for instance, to say nothing of such fashionable figures as MM. Zuloaga *et* Sert. There he will find better Dutchmen than Van Dongen, and an active colony of Scandinavians the most interesting of whom is probably Per Krohg. The career of Krohg, by the way, is worth considering for a moment and watching for the future. Finely gifted in many ways, he started work under three crippling disabilities —a literary imagination, natural facility, and inherited science. The results were at first precisely what might have been expected. Now, however, he is getting the upper hand of his unlucky equipment; and his genuine talent and personal taste, beginning to assert themselves, have made it impossible for criticism any longer to treat him merely as an amiable member of a respectable group. What is true of Spain and Scandinavia is even truer of Poland and what remains of Russia. Goncharova and Larionoff—the former a typically temperamental artist, the latter an extravagantly doctrinaire one—Soudcikine, Grigorieff, Zadkine live permanently in Paris; while Kisling, whom I take to be the best of the Poles, has become so completely identified with the country in which he lives, and for which he fought, that he is often taken by English critics for a Frenchman. Survage (with his eccentric but sure sense of colour), Soutine (with his delicious paint), and Marcoussis (a cubist of great merit) each, in his own way, working in Paris, adds to the artistic reputation of his native country. In the rue La Boëtie you can see the work of painters and sculptors from every country in Europe almost, and from a good many in Africa. The Italian Futurists have often made exhibitions there. While the work of Severini—their most creditable representative—is always to be found *chez* Léonce Rosenberg, hard by in the rue de la Baume.

However, most of the Futurists have retired to their own country, where we will leave them. On the other hand, the most gifted Italian painter who has appeared this century, Modigliani, was bred on the Boulevard Montparnasse. In the movement he occupies an intermediate position, being neither of the pioneers nor yet of the post-war generation. He was not much heard of before the war,* and he died less than a year after peace was signed. In my mind, therefore, his name is associated with the war—then, at any rate, was the hour of his glory ; he dominated the cosmopolitan groups of his quarter at a time when most of the French painters, masters and disciples, were in the trenches. Modigliani owed something to Cézanne and a great deal to Picasso : he was no doctrinaire : towards

* He was at work, however, by 1906—perhaps earlier.

the end he became the slave of a formula of his own devising——but that is another matter. Modigliani had an intense but narrow sensibility, his music is all on one string : he had a characteristically Italian gift for drawing beautifully with ease : and I think he had not much else. I feel sure that those who would place him amongst the masters of the movement—— Matisse, Picasso, Derain, Bonnard, and Friesz ——mistake ; for, with all his charm and originality, he was too thoughtless and superficial to achieve greatly. He invented something which he went on repeating ; and he could always fascinate simply by his way of handling a brush or a pencil. His pictures, delightful and surprising at first sight, are apt to grow stale and, in the end, some of them, unbearably thin. A minor artist, surely.

Though Paris is unquestionably the centre of the movement, no one who sees only what comes thither and to London——and that is all I see——can have much idea of what is going on in Germany and America. Germany has not yet recommenced sending her art in quantities that make judgement possible, while it is pretty clear that the American art which reaches Europe is by no means the best that America can do. From both come magazines with photographs which excite our curiosity, but on such evidence it would be mere impertinence to form an opinion. Of contemporary art in

Germany and America I shall say nothing.
And what shall I say of the home-grown
article ? Having taken Paris for my point of
view, I am excused from saying much. Not
much of English art is seen from Paris. We
have but one living painter whose work is at all
well known to the serious amateurs of that
city, and he is Sickert.* The name, however,
of Augustus John is often pronounced, ill—
for they *will* call him Augustin—and that of
Steer is occasionally murmured. Through the
salon d'automne Roger Fry is becoming known ;
and there is a good deal of curiosity about the
work of Duncan Grant, and some about that
of Mark Gertler and Vanessa Bell. Now, of
these, Sickert and Steer are essentially, and in
no bad sense, provincial masters. They are
belated impressionists of considerable merit
working in a thoroughly fresh and personal
way on the problems of a bygone age. In
the remoter parts of Europe as late as the
beginning of the seventeenth century were to
be found genuine and interesting artists working in the Gothic tradition : the existence of
Sickert and Steer made us realize how far from

* The Irish painter O'Conor, and the Canadian Morrice,
are both known and respected in Paris; but because they
have lived their lives there and known none but French influences they are rarely thought of as British. In a less
degree the same might be said of that admirable painter
George Barne.

the centre is London still. On the Continent such conservatism would almost certainly be the outcome of stupidity or prejudice; but both Sickert and Steer have still something of their own to say about the world seen through an impressionist temperament. The prodigious reputation enjoyed by Augustus John is another sign of our isolation. His splendid talent when, as a young man, he took it near enough the central warmth to make it expand (besides the influence of Puvis, remember, it underwent that of Picasso) began to bear flowers of delicious promise. Had he kept it there John might never have tasted the sweets of insular renown: he would have had his place in the history of painting, however. The French know enough of Vorticism to know that it is a provincial and utterly insignificant contrivance which has borrowed what it could from Cubism and Futurism and added nothing to either. They like to fancy that the English tradition is that of Gainsborough and Constable, quite failing to realize what havoc has been made of this admirable plastic tradition by that puerile gospel of literary pretentiousness called Pre-Raphaelism. Towards these mournful quags and quicksands, with their dead-sea flora of anecdote and allegory, the best part of the little talent we produce seems irresistibly to be drawn: by these at last it is sucked down.

That, at any rate, is the way that most of those English artists who ten or a dozen years ago gave such good promise have gone. Let us hope better of the new generation—recent exhibitions afford some excuse—a generation which, if reactionarily inclined, can always take Steer for a model, or, if disposed to keep abreast of the times and share in the heritage of Cézanne as well as that of Constable, can draw courage from the fact that there is, after all, one English painter—Duncan Grant—who takes honourable rank beside the best of his contemporaries.

It is fifteen years since Cézanne died, and only now is it becoming possible to criticize him. That shows how overwhelming his influence was. The fact that at last his admirers and disciples, no longer under any spell or distorting sense of loyalty, recognize that there are in painting plenty of things worth doing which he never did is all to the good. It is now possible to criticize him seriously ; and when all his insufficiencies have been fairly shown he remains one of the very greatest painters that ever lived. The serious criticism of Cézanne is a landmark in the history of the movement, and still something of a novelty ; for, naturally, I reckon the vulgar vituperation with which his work was greeted, and the faint praise with which it was subsequently damned, as no criticism at all. The hacks and pedagogues and middle-class metaphysicians who abused him, and only when it dawned on them that they were making themselves silly, in the eyes of their own flock even, took to patronizing, are forgot. They babble in the Burlington Fine Arts Club—where nobody marks them—and have their reward in professorships and the direction of public galleries. The criticism that matters, of which we are beginning to hear something, comes mostly from painters, his ardent admirers, who realize that Cézanne attempted things which he failed to achieve and deliberately shunned others worth achieving. Also, they realize that there is always a danger of one good custom corrupting the world.

Cézanne is the full-stop between impressionism and the contemporary movement. Of course there is really no such thing as a full-stop in art any more than there is in nature. Movement grows out of movement, and every artist is attached to the past by a thousand binders springing from a thousand places in the great stem of tradition. But it is true that there is hardly one modern artist of importance to whom Cézanne is not father or grandfather, and that no other influence is comparable with his. To be sure there is Seurat, of whom we shall hear more in the next ten years. Although he died as long ago as 1891 his importance has not yet been fully realized, his discoveries have not been fully exploited, not yet has his extraordinary genius received adequate recognition. Seurat may be the Giorgione of the movement. Working in isolation and dying young, he is known to us only by a few pictures which reveal unmistakeable and mysterious genius ; but I should not be surprised if from the next generation he were to receive honours equal almost to those paid Cézanne.

The brave *douanier* was hardly master enough to have great and enduring influence ; nevertheless, the sincerity of his vision and directness of his method reinforced and even added to one part of the lesson taught by Cézanne : also, it was he who—by his pictures, not by doctrine of course—sent the pick of the young generation to look at the primitives. Such as it was, his influence was a genuinely plastic one, which is more, I think, than can be said for that of Gauguin or of Van Gogh. The former seemed wildly exciting for a moment, partly because he flattened out his forms, designed in two dimensions, and painted without chiaroscuro in pure colours, but even more because he had very much the air of a rebel. " Il nous faut les barbares," said André Gide ; " il nous faut les barbares," said we all. Well, here was someone who had gone to live with them, and sent home thrilling, and often very beautiful, pictures which could, if one chose, be taken as challenges to European civilization.

SINCE CÉZANNE

To a considerable extent the influence of Gauguin was literary, and therefore in the long run negligible. It is a mistake on that account to suppose—as many seem inclined to do—that Gauguin was not a fine painter.

Van Gogh was a fine painter, too ; but his influence, like that of Gauguin, has proved nugatory—a fact which detracts nothing from the merit of his work. He was fitted by his admirers into current social and political tendencies, and coupled with Charles-Louis Philippe as an apostle of sentimental anarchy. Sentimental portraits of washerwomen and artisans were compared with Marie Donadieu and Bubu de Montparnasse ; and by indiscreet enthusiasm the artist was degraded to the level of a preacher. Nor was this degradation inexcusable : Van Gogh was a preacher, and too often his delicious and sensitive works of art are smeared over, to their detriment, with tendencious propaganda. At his best, however, he is a very great impressionist—a neo-impressionist, or expressionist if you like—but I should say an impressionist much influenced and much to the good, as was Gauguin, by acquaintance with Cézanne in his last and most instructive phase. Indeed, it is clear that Gauguin and Van Gogh would not have come near achieving what they did achieve—achieved, mind you, as genuine painters—had they not been amongst the first to realize and make use of that bewildering revelation which is the art of Cézanne.

Of that art I am not here to speak ; I am concerned only with its influence. Taking the thing at its roughest and simplest, one may say that the influence of Cézanne during the last seventeen years has manifested itself most obviously in two characteristics—Directness and what is called Distortion. Cézanne was direct because he set himself a task which admitted of no adscititious flourishes—the creation of form which should be entirely self-supporting and intrinsically significant, *la possession de la forme* as his descendants call it now. To this great end all means were good: all that was not a means to this end was superfluous. To achieve it he was prepared to play the oddest tricks with natural forms—to distort. All great artists have distorted; Cézanne was peculiar only in doing so more consciously and thoroughly than most. What is important in his art is, of course, the beauty of his conceptions and his power in pursuit : indifference to verisimilitude is but the outward and visible sign of this inward and spiritual grace. For some, however, though not for most of his followers his distortion had an importance of its own.

To the young painters of 1904, or thereabouts, Cézanne came as the liberator : he it was who had freed painting from a mass of

conventions which, useful once, had grown
old and stiff and were now no more than so
many impediments to expression. To most
of them his chief importance—as an influence,
of course—was that he had removed all unnecessary barriers between what they felt and
its realization in form. It was his directness
that was thrilling. But to an important
minority the distortions and simplifications—
the reduction of natural forms to spheres,
cylinders, cones, etc.—which Cézanne had
used as means were held to be in themselves
of consequence because capable of fruitful
development. From them it was found possible to deduce a theory of art—a complete
æsthetic even. Put on a fresh track by
Cézanne's practice, a group of gifted and
thoughtful painters began to speculate on the
nature of form and its appeal to the æsthetic
sense, and not to speculate only, but to materialize their speculations. The greatest of them,
Picasso, invented Cubism. If I call these
artists who forged themselves a theory of form
and used it as a means of expression Doctrinaires it is because to me that name bears
no disparaging implication and seems to indicate well enough what I take to be their one
common characteristic : if I call those who,
without giving outward sign (they may well
have had their private speculations and systems)
of an abstract theory, appeared to use distor-

tion when, where, and as their immediate sensibility dictated, Fauves, that is because the word has passed into three languages, is admirably colourless—for all its signifying a colour—and implies the existence of a group without specifying a peculiarity. Into Doctrinaires—Theorists if you like the word better—and Fauves the first generation of Cézanne's descendants could, I feel sure, be divided ; whether such a division would serve any useful purpose is another matter. What I am sure of is that to have two such labels, to be applied when occasion requires and cancelled without much compunction, will excellently serve mine, which may, or may not, be useful.

I would not insist too strongly on the division ; certainly at first it was not felt to be sharp. Plenty of Fauves did their whack of theorizing, while some of the theorists are amongst the most sensitive and personal of the age. What I do insist on—because it explains and excuses the character of my book— is that in this age theory has played so prominent a part, hardly one artist of importance quite escaping its influence, that no critic who proposes to give some account of painting since Cézanne can be expected to overlook it : some, to be sure, may be thought to have stared indecently. The division between Fauves and Theorists, I was saying, in the beginning was not sharp ; nevertheless, because it was

real, already in the first generation of Cézanne's
descendants the seeds of two schools were
sown. Already by 1910 two tendencies are
visibly distinct; but up to 1914, though there
is divergence, there is, I think, no antipathy
between them—of antipathies between in-
dividuals I say nothing. Solidarity was imposed on the young generation by the virulent
and not over scrupulous hostility of the old;
it was *l'union sacrée* in face of the enemy.
And just as political allies are apt to become
fully alive to the divergence of their aims and
ambitions only after they have secured their
position by victory, so it was not until the new
movement had been recognized by all educated
people as representative and dominant that the
Fauves felt inclined to give vent to their inevitable dislike of Doctrinaires.

Taken as a whole, the first fourteen years of
the century, which my malicious friend Jean
Cocteau sometimes calls *l'époque héroïque*, possessed most of the virtues and vices that such
an epoch should possess. It was rich in fine
artists; and these artists were finely prolific.
It was experimental, and passionate in its experiments. It was admirably disinterested.
Partly from the pressure of opposition, partly
because the family characteristics of the Cézan-
nides are conspicuous, it acquired a rather
deceptive air of homogeneity. It was inclined
to accept recruits without scrutinizing over

closely their credentials, though it is to be remembered that it kept its critical faculty sufficiently sharp to reject the Futurists while welcoming the Cubists. I cannot deny, however, that in that moment of enthusiasm and loyalty we were rather disposed to find extraordinary merits in commonplace painters. We knew well enough that a feeble and incompetent disciple of Cézanne was just as worthless as a feeble and incompetent disciple of anyone else —but, then, was our particular postulant so feeble after all ? Also, we were fond of arguing that the liberating influence of Cézanne had made it possible for a mediocre artist to express a little store of recondite virtue which under another dispensation must have lain hid for ever. I doubt we exaggerated. We were much too kind, I fancy, to a number of perfectly commonplace young people, and said a number of foolish things about them. What was worse, we were unjust to the past. That was inevitable. The intemperate ferocity of the opposition drove us into Protestantism, and Protestantism is unjust always. It made us narrow, unwilling to give credit to outsiders of merit, and grossly indulgent to insiders of little or none. Certainly we appreciated the Orientals, the Primitives, and savage art as they had never been appreciated before ; but we underrated the art of the Renaissance and of the eighteenth and nineteenth centuries.

Also, because we set great store by our theories and sought their implications everywhere, we claimed kinship with a literary movement with which, in fact, we had nothing in common. Charles-Louis Philippe and the Unanimistes should never have been compared with the descendants of Cézanne. Happily, when it came to dragging in Tolstoyism, and Dostoievskyism even, and making of the movement something moral and political almost, the connection was seen to be ridiculous and was duly cut.

The protagonists of the heroic epoch (1904–1914 shall we say?) were Matisse and Picasso. In modern European painting Picasso remains the paramount influence; of modern French, however, Derain is the chief; while Matisse, who may still be the best painter alive, has hardly any influence at all. In these early days Derain, considerably younger than Matisse and less precocious than Picasso, was less conspicuous than either; yet he always held a peculiar and eminent position, with an intellect apt for theoretical conundrums and sensibility to match that of any Fauve and his personal genius brooding over both. About the best known of Matisse's companions—for they were in no sense his disciples—were, I should say, Friesz, Vlaminck, Laprade, Chabaud, Marquet, Manguin, Puy, Delaunay, Rouault, Girieud, Flandrin. I think I am justified in describing all these, with the exception, perhaps, of Girieud and Flandrin, as Fauves ; assuredly I have heard them all so described. In very early days Maurice Denis was by some reckoned a chief, the equal almost of Matisse ; but through sloppy sentiment he fell into mere futility, and by now has quite dropped out. Friesz, on the other hand, has gone ahead, and is to-day one of the half-dozen leaders : I shall have a good deal to say about him in a later part of this book. Vlaminck a few years ago had the misfortune to learn a recipe for making attractive and sparkling pictures ; he is now, I understand, in retirement trying to unlearn it. Rouault is a very interesting artist of whom we see little ; from what I have seen I should be inclined to fear that a taste for romance and drama is too often suffered to smother his remarkable gift for painting. Marquet, with gifts equal to almost anything, is content, it seems, to remain a brilliant but superficial impressionist. Puy is a thoroughly sound artist, and so in a smaller way is Manguin. What has become of Chabaud, who was a bit too clever, and a little vulgar even ? And what of Delaunay ? And of Flandrin—what has become of him ? Something sufficiently interesting, at any rate, to give pause even to a critic in a hurry. His name must not go by unmarked. Flandrin was amongst the first to rebel against Impressionism—against that impressionism, I mean, which remained implicit in post-impressionism. Resolutely he set his face against the prevailing habit of expressing an aspect of things, and tried hard to make a picture. So far he has succeeded imperfectly : but he is still trying.

Of one artist who is certainly no Doctrinaire, nor yet, I think, a Fauve, but who has been influenced by Cézanne, I shall here do myself the honour of pronouncing the name. Aristide Maillol is so obviously the best sculptor alive that to people familiar with his work there is something comic about those discussions in which are canvassed the claims of Mestrovic and Epstein, Archipenko and Bourdelle. These have their merits ; but Maillol is a great artist. He works in the classical tradition, modified by Cézanne, thanks largely to whom, I imagine, he has freed himself from the impressionism— the tiresome agitation and emphasis—of Rodin. He has founded no school ; but one pupil of his, Gimon—a very young sculptor—deserves watching. From the doctrine a small but interesting school of sculpture has come : Laurens, an artist of sensibility and some power, and Lipsitz are its most admired representatives. At home we have Epstein and Dobson ; both have been through the stern school of abstract construction, and Epstein has emerged the most brilliant *pasticheur* alive.

Brancuzi (a Bohemian) is, I should say, by temperament more Fauve than Doctrinaire. Older than most of Cézanne's descendants, he has nevertheless been profoundly influenced by the master ; but the delicacy of his touch, which gives sometimes to his modelling almost the quality of Wei sculpture, he learnt from no one—such things not being taught. Gaudier Brzcska, a young French sculptor of considerable promise, was killed in the early months of the war. He had been living in England, where his work, probably on account of its manifest superiority to most of what was seen near it, gained an exaggerated reputation. The promise was indisputable ; but, after seeing the Leicester Gallery exhibition, I came to the conclusion that there was not much else. Indeed, his drawings often betrayed so superficial a facility, such a turn for calligraphic dexterities, that one began to wonder whether even in expecting much one had not been over sanguine. The extravagant reputation enjoyed by Gaudier in this country will perhaps cross the mind of anyone who happens to read my essay on Wilcoxism : native, or even resident, geese look uncommonly like swans on home waters : to see them as they are you should see them abroad.

Bonnard and Vuillard, unlike Aristide Maillol, though being sensitive and intelligent artists who make the most of whatever serves their turn they have taken what they wanted from the atmosphere in which they work, are hardly to be counted of Cézanne's descendants. Rather are they children of the great impressionists who, unlike the majority of their surviving brothers and sisters, instead of swallowing the impressionist doctrine whole, just as official painters do the academic, have modified it charmingly to suit their peculiar temperaments. Not having swallowed the poker, they have none of those stiff and static habits which characterize the later generations of their family. They are free and various; and Bonnard is one of the greatest painters alive. Mistakenly, he is supposed to have influenced Duncan Grant; but Duncan Grant, at the time when he was painting pictures which appear to have certain affinities with those of Bonnard, was wholly unacquainted with the work of that master. On the other hand, it does seem possible that Vuillard has influenced another English painter, Miss Ethel Sands: only, in making attributions of influence one cannot be too careful. About direct affiliations especially, as this case shows, one should never be positive. It is as probable that Miss Sands has been influenced by Sickert, who has much in common with Vuillard, as by Vuillard himself; and most probable of all, perhaps, that the three have inherited from a common ancestor something which each has developed and cultivated as seemed to him or her best. *La recherche de la paternité* was ever an exciting but hazardous pastime : if Bonnard and Vuillard, in their turn, are claimed, as they sometimes are, for descendants of Renoir, with equal propriety Sickert may be claimed for Degas. And it is worth noting, perhaps, as a curious fact, that in the matter of influence this is about as much as at the moment can be claimed for either of these masters. Both Renoir and Degas lived well on into the period of which I am writing ; but though both were admired, the former immensely, neither up to the present has had much direct influence on contemporary painting.

From 1908—I choose that year to avoid all risk of ante-dating—there existed side by side, and apparently in alliance, with the Fauves a school of theoretical painters. Of Cubism I have said my say elsewhere : if I have some doubts as to whether, as a complete theory of painting, it has a future, I have none that what it has already achieved is remarkable. Also, I recognize its importance as a school of experiments, some of which are sure to bear fruit and leave a mark on history. Of the merits of many of its professors I say nothing, because they are manifest and admitted. Picasso stands apart : he is the inventor and most eminent exponent, yet I refuse to call him Cubist because he is so many other things.

Braque, who at present confines himself to abstractions, and to taste and sensibility adds creative power, is to my mind the best of the bunch : while Léger, Gris, Gleizes, and Metzinger are four painters who, if they did not limit themselves to a means of expression which to most people is still perplexing, if not disagreeable, would be universally acclaimed for what they are—four exceptionally inventive artists, each possessing his own peculiar and precious sense of colour and design.

But besides these pure doctrinaires there were a good many painters who, without reducing their forms to geometrical abstractions, by modifying them in accordance with Cubist theory gave a new and impressive coherence to their compositions. Of them the best known, in England at all events, is Jean Marchand, whose admirable work has been admired here ever since the Grafton Galleries exhibition of 1912. Lately he has moved away from Cubism, but has not become less doctrinaire for that. Indeed, if I have a fault to find with his grave and masterly art it is that sometimes it is a little wanting in sensibility and inspiration. Marchand is so determined to paint logically and well that he seems a little to forget that in the greatest art there is more than logic and good painting. It is odd to remember that Lhote, who since the war has been saluted by a band of young painters (not French for the most part, I believe) as chief of a new and profoundly doctrinaire school which is to reconcile Cubism with the great tradition, stood at the time of which I am writing pretty much where Marchand stood. His undeniable gifts, which have not failed him since, were then devoted to combining the amusing qualities of the *imagiers* (popular print-makers) with the new discoveries. The results were consistently pleasing ; and I will here confess that, however little I may like some of his later preaching and however little he may like mine, what Lhote produces in paint never fails to arrest me and very seldom to charm. Herbin, who was another of those who about the year 1910 were modifying natural forms in obedience to Cubist theory, has since gone all lengths in the direction of pure abstraction : his art is none the better for it. Valloton, so far as I can remember, was much where Herbin was. Now apparently he aims at the grand tragic ; an aim which rarely fails to lead its votaries by way of the grand academic. Perhaps such aspirations can express themselves only in the consecrated formulæ of traditional rhetoric ; at all events, the last I saw of Valloton was furiously classical.* And for all that he re-

---

* His exhibits in the *salon d'automne* of 1921, however, suggest that he has come off his high horse.

mains, what he was in the beginning, an illustrator.

To me these artists all seem to be of the first generation of Cézanne's descendants. About the dates of one or two, however, I may well be mistaken ; and so may I be when I suppose half a dozen more of whose existence I became aware rather later—only a year or two before the war, in fact—to be of a slightly later brood. For instance, it must have been at the end of 1912, or the beginning of 1913, that I first heard of Modigliani, Utrillo, Segonzac, Marie Laurencin, Luc-Albert Moreau and Kisling, though doubtless all were known earlier to wide-awake men on the spot. None of them can fairly be described as doctrinaire : by that time an artist with a pronounced taste for abstractions betook himself to Cubism almost as a matter of course. All owe much to Cézanne—Utrillo least; Modigliani and Marie Laurencin owe a good deal to Picasso's blue period ; while Luc-Albert Moreau owes something to Segonzac. Of the two first Modigliani is dead and Utrillo so ill that he is unlikely ever to paint again.* A strange artist, Utrillo, personal enough, just as Modigliani was handsome enough, to satisfy the exigences of the most romantic melodrama, with a touch

* With great pleasure I contradict this. According to latest reports Utrillo is so far recovered that before long he may be painting again.

of madness and an odd nostalgic passion—expressing itself in an inimitable white—for the dank and dirty whitewash and cheap cast-iron of the Parisian suburbs. Towards the end, when he was already very ill, he began to concoct a formula for dealing with these melancholy scenes which might have been his undoing. His career was of a few years only, but those years were prolific; beginning in a rather old-fashioned, impressionistic style, he soon found his way into the one he has made famous. To judge his art as a whole is difficult: partly because his early productions are not only unequal to, but positively unlike, what he achieved later; partly because many of the Utrillos with which Paris is overstocked were painted by someone else.

Perhaps the most interesting, though neither the most startling nor seductive, of this batch is Segonzac. Like all the best things in nature, he matures slowly and gets a little riper every day; so, as he is already a thoroughly good painter, like the nigger of Saint-Cyr he has but to continue. Before nature, or rather cultivation, with its chocolate ploughed fields and bright green trees, as before the sumptuous splendours of a naked body, his reaction is manifestly, flutteringly, lyrical. He might have been a bucolic rhapsodist had not his sensibility been well under the control of as sound a head as you would expect to find on

28

the shoulders of a gentleman of Gascony. His emotions are kept severely in their place by rigorous concentration on the art of painting. Nevertheless, there are critics who complain that his compositions still tend to lack organization and his forms definition. And perhaps they do sometimes : only in these, as in other respects, his art improves steadily.*

" Sa peinture a un petit côté vicieux qui est adorable "—I have heard the phrase so often that I can but repeat it. Marie Laurencin's painting is adorable ; we can never like her enough for liking her own femininity so well, and for showing all her charming talent instead of smothering it in an effort to paint like a man ; but she is not a great artist— she is not even the best woman painter alive. She is barely as good as Dufy (a contemporary of Picasso unless I mistake, but for many years known rather as a decorator and illustrator than a painter in oils) who, while he confined himself to designing for the upholsterers and making " images," was very good indeed. His oil-paintings are another matter. Dufy has a formula for making pictures ; he has a cliché for a tree, a house, a chimney, even for the smoke coming out of a chimney. In this way he can be sure of producing a pretty article, and, what is more, an article the public likes.

---

* *Salon d'automne,* 1921 : It has again made a big stride forward. Segonzac is now amongst the best painters in France.

Very different is the art of Kisling. Rarely does he produce one of those pictures so appetizing that one fancies they must be good to eat. What you will find in his work, besides much good painting, is a serious preoccupation with the problem of externalizing in form an æsthetic experience. And as, after all, that is the proper end of art his work is treated with respect by all the best painters and most understanding critics, though it has not yet scored a popular success. "Kisling ne triche pas," says André Salmon.

The war did not kill the movement : none but a fool could have supposed that it would. Nevertheless, it had one ghastly effect on contemporary painting. When I returned to Paris in the autumn of 1919 I found the painters whom I had known before the war developing, more or less normally, and producing work which fell nowise short of what one had come to expect. I saw all that there was to be seen ; I admired ; and then I asked one who had already, before the war, established a style and a reputation—I asked Friesz, I think—" Et les jeunes ? " " Nous sommes les jeunes " was the reply. Those young French painters who should have been emerging from the ruck of students between 1914 and 1919 had either been killed, or deflected from their career, or gravely retarded. Only now is *la jeunesse* beginning to give signs of vitality ;

only now is a new crop coming to the surface ;
so now I will take the foolhardy risk of pronouncing the names of a few who seem to me
to have given proof of undeniable talent—
Gabriel-Fournier, Favory, Lotiron, Soutine,
Corneau, Durey, Monzain, Richard, Guindet,
Togores, Gromaire, Alix, Halicka. I must
not be taken to assert that all of these are under
thirty, or that none was known to discerning
amateurs before the war, or in its first years
at any rate. Certainly, the work of Gabriel-
Fournier, Favory, Soutine, and I think of
Corneau, was known to me even, through photographs, before the Armistice was signed. As certainly I think it is true that all are of a later crop
than Segonzac, Marie Laurencin, Luc-Albert
Moreau, etc., while Monzain, Richard, Togores, Gromaire, Alix, Guindet, and Halicka
are very young indeed. So here are a dozen
painters—most of them little known at present
outside a smallish circle of artists, critics, and inquisitive amateurs—who appear to give promise
of excellence : amongst them I should be inclined
to look for the masters of a coming age.*

* Twelve years ago I made a list of young or youngish
painters—the men of thirty or thereabouts—from whom it
seemed to me reasonable to expect great things. It included
such names as Derain, Picasso, Vlaminck, Marchand,
Friesz, Maillol, Duncan Grant : one need not be *laudator
temporis acti* to feel that the men of the new generation are
on a smaller scale. This merely confirms my often expressed
notion that the decade 1875–85 produced a prodigious

To this list I would add, in no spirit of
paradox, two names which, at first sight, must
appear singularly out of place—Camoin and
Guérin. Both were at work before the contemporary movement—the Cézanne movement—was born or, at any rate, launched ;
both for a long time seemed to be, if anything,
opposed to it ; both for some years lay dormant
in a chrysalis-like state to emerge recently a
pair of very interesting painters. The Camoin
and the Guérin with whom I am concerned
appeared since the war ; they may, of course,
relapse into their former condition : time will
show. Apparently it was only three or four
years ago that Camoin realized that Matisse—
his contemporary—was the master from whom
he could draw that nourishment which one

quantity of greatly gifted babies. On the other hand, if by
comparison with the *salon d'automne* of 1911 that of '21
seems unexciting, we must not fail to do justice to the
extraordinarily high level of painting that has now been
attained. And this confirms another of my pet theories—
that we live in an age comparable (so far as painting goes)
with the *quattro cento*. The works of even the smallest artists
of that age enchant us now, because in that age any man of
any talent could make a picture; but doubtless at the time
critics and amateurs sighed for the first thrilling years of the
movement—for the discoveries of Masaccio and Donatello—
and were quite ready to welcome the novelties of the high
renaissance when they came. The world moves faster nowadays; already we look regretfully back to the days when
Matisse and Picasso were launching the movement, and
another high renaissance may be nearer than we suppose.

good artist may very legitimately draw from another. So nourished, he seems to have made a fresh start ; at any rate his work has now a freshness and vivacity which in his younger days he could never impart. The case of Guérin is odder still. A passionate admirer of Watteau, he would seem to have locked himself up in a rather sterile devotion to the eighteenth century master. One must suppose that there was something dead in his appreciation, something recognized but unfelt, and therefore not really understood. This deadness came through into his work. Lacking genuine inspiration, struggling in consequence to impart life by tricks and conventions, he occasionally allowed himself to tumble into downright vulgarity. Suddenly, and without renouncing any ancient loyalty, he has come to life. It is Watteau that inspires him still ; but the essential Watteau—Watteau the painter —not that superficies which is more or less familiar to every hack, be he limner or penman, who dabbles in the eighteenth century. How amusing to fancy that the just admiration now felt for the genius of Watteau by those descendants of Cézanne who formerly misesteemed it has somehow put Guérin himself in the way of becoming intimate with an art he had formerly worshipped at a distance!

Though the war did not kill or even cripple the movement, since the war there has been a change, or, at any rate, a change has become apparent. To begin with, Picasso has, in a sense, retired from public life—from the life of the *cafés* and studios I mean—and in isolation works out those problems that are for ever presenting themselves to his restless brain. The splendid fruit of his solitude we saw last summer *chez* Paul Rosenberg. From time to time Picasso still paints a Cubist picture—to keep his mind in—but he is hardly to be reckoned a Cubist, and certainly not a pure one. Of that school, which still flourishes (exhibiting at *la Section d'Or* or rue de la Baume the work of Braque, Gleizes, Léger, Metzinger, Gris, Laurens, Lipsitz, Marcoussis, Henry Hayden, and the brilliant Irène Lagut), Picasso is the inspiration, perhaps, but not the chief. His influence in the western world and on foreign painters in Paris is as great as ever ; but the French, slightly vexed, maybe, at having accepted so long the leadership of a Spaniard, show signs of turning back towards their national tradition. So, though Picasso remains the animator of the doctrinaire school or schools, Lhote may become the master. It is the fashion, I know, not to take his influence seriously. No matter how clever a man he may be, Lhote—they say—is not a big enough painter to be a chief. It may be so —I suspect it is—yet we should not forget that, besides being intelligent and capable of drawing more or less plausible inferences from premises of his own choosing, Lhote can point to a practice by no means despicable. For the rest, he is the apostle of logic and discipline, and so finds plenty to approve in the Cubist doctrine and the French tradition from Poussin to David. I do not know whether Bissière is to be ranked amongst his disciples—I should think not— but Bissière, a most attractive artist, is perhaps significant of the new tendency in that he has chosen to express a whimsical temperament in terms of prim science. About the science of picture-making, as the director of the National Gallery calls it, he has little to learn. He knows the masters, the Primitives especially, and has a way, at once logical and fantastic, of playing on their *motifs* which gives sometimes the happiest results. Bissière is too fanciful and odd ever to be a *chef d'école* or representative even; but the very fact that, being what he is, he has chosen such means of expression is symptomatic.

So the doctrinaire side of the movement persists, animated by Picasso, and schooled to some extent by Lhote. The main current, however, has found another channel; and, unless I mistake, we are already in the second phase of the movement—a phase in which the revelations of Cézanne and Seurat and the elaborations of their immediate descendants will be modified and revitalized by the pressure and spirit of the great tradition. The leader has already been chosen. Derain is the chief of the new French school—a school destined manifestly to be less cosmopolitan than its predecessor. The tendency towards nationalism everywhere is unmistakeable—a consequence of the war, I suppose. It is useless to deplore the fact or exult in it : one can but accept it as one accepts the weather. Even England has not escaped ; and it is to be noted that our best painter, Duncan Grant, a descendant of Cézanne who has run the whole gamut of abstract experiment, is settling down, without of course for a moment denying his master, to exploit the French heritage, with feet planted firmly in the English tradition— the tradition of Gainsborough and Constable. In France, where tradition is so much richer, its weight will confine more closely and drive more intensely the new spirit. One new tendency—that which insists more passionately than ever on order and organization—merely continues the impetus given by Cézanne and received by all his followers; but another, more vague, towards something which I had rather call humanism than humanity, does imply, I think, a definite breach with Cubism and the tenets of the austerer doctrinaires. It is not drama or anecdote or sentiment or symbolism that this would bring back to the plastic arts, but rather that mysterious yet recognizable quality in which the art of Raffael excels—a calm, disinterested, and professional concern with the significance of life as revealed directly in form, a faint desire, perhaps, to touch by a picture, a building, or a simple object of use some curious over-tone of our æsthetic sense. Deep in their quest of that borderland beauty which is common to life and art French painters are once again deeply concerned with life : to borrow an idea from my next essay, thay have chosen a new artistic problem. To them, however, " life " does not mean what it means to the sentimentalists or melodramatists, nor even precisely what it meant to the Impressionists. Contemporary French painting has no taste for contemporary actualities. By " life " it understands, not what is going on in the street, but—what to be sure does go on there because it goes on everywhere—the thing that poets used to call " the animating spark." About life, in that sense, the painters of the new generation will, I fancy, have something to say. They will come at it, not by drama or anecdote or symbol, but, as all genuine artists have always come at whatever possessed their imaginations, by plastic expression, or—if you like old-fashioned phrases—by creating significant form. They will seek the vital principle in all sorts of objects and translate it into forms of every kind. That humane beauty after which Derain strives is to be found, I said, in Raffael : it is to be found also in the Parthenon.

I think this preliminary essay should close, as it began, on a note of humility and with an explanation. Twenty years ago, when I was an undergraduate, I remember reading just after it was published M. Camille Mauclair's little book on the Impressionists. Long ago I ceased much to admire M. Mauclair's writing : his theorizing and pseudo-science now strike me as silly, and his judgements seem lacking in perspicacity. But whatever I may think of it now I shall not forget what I owe that book. Even at Cambridge the spirit of the age, which is said to pervade the air like a pestilence, had infected me ; and I set out on my first visit to Paris full of curiosity about what was then the contemporary movement—at its last gasp. My guide was M. Mauclair ; his book it was that put me in the right way. For by bringing me acquainted with current theories and reputations, and by throwing me into a fever of expectation, he brought my æsthetic sensibilities to that state in which they reacted swiftly and generously to the pictures themselves. This, as I shall explain in another essay, is, to my mind, the proper function of criticism. I shall never forget my first visits to the Caillebotte collection ; and in the unforgettable thrill of those first visits M. Mauclair's bad science and erratic judgement counted for something—much perhaps. They put me into a mood of sympathetic expectation; and such a mood is, even for highly sensitive people, often an indispensable preliminary to æsthetic appreciation. There are those who have got to be made to feel before they can begin to feel for themselves— believe me, they are not the least sensitive or genuine of amateurs : they are only the most honest. I should like very much to do for even one of them what M. Mauclair did for me. It would be delightful to believe that by putting him in the way of the best modern painting and the theories concerning or connected with it—theories which, it seems, for some make it more intelligible—I was giving his sensibility a serviceable jog. Everyone, I know, must see with his own eyes and feel through his own nerves ; none can lend another eyes or emotions : nevertheless, one can point and gesticulate and in so doing excite. If I have done that I am content. Twenty years hence, it is to be presumed, those who now read my writings will be saying of them what I was saying of M. Mauclair's. The prospect does not distress me. I am not author enough to be pained by the certainty that in ten years' time this book will be obsolete. Like M. Mauclair's, it will have served its turn ; and I make no doubt there will be someone at hand to write another, the same in purpose, and in execution let us hope rather neater.

THE ARTISTIC PROBLEM

We all agree now—by "we" I mean intelligent people under sixty—that a work of art is like a rose. A rose is not beautiful because it is like something else. Neither is a work of art. Roses and works of art are beautiful in themselves. Unluckily, the matter does not end there : a rose is the visible result of an infinitude of complicated goings on in the bosom of the earth and in the air above, and similarly a work of art is the product of strange activities in the human mind. In so far as we are mere spectators and connoisseurs we need not bother about these ; all we are concerned with is the finished product, the work of art. To produce the best eggs it may be that hens should be fed on hot meal mash. That is a question for the farmer. For us what matters is the quality of the eggs, since it is them and not hot meal mash that we propose to eat for breakfast. Few, however, can take quite so lordly an attitude towards art. We contemplate the object, we experience the appropriate emotion, and then we begin asking "Why?" and "How?" Personally, I am so conscious of these insistent questions that, at the risk of some misunderstanding, I habitually describe works of art as " significant " rather than " beautiful " forms. For works of art, unlike roses, are the creations and expressions of conscious minds. I beg that no theological

40

red herring may here be drawn across the scent.

A work of art is an object beautiful, or significant, in itself, nowise dependent for its value on the outside world, capable by itself of provoking in us that emotion which we call æsthetic. Agreed. But men do not create such things unconsciously and without effort, as they breathe in their sleep. On the contrary, for their production are required special energies and a peculiar state of mind. A work of art, like a rose, is the result of a string of causes : and some of us are so vain as to take more interest in the operations of the human mind than in fertilizers and watering-pots.

In the pre-natal history of a work of art I seem to detect at any rate three factors—a state of peculiar and intense sensibility, the creative impulse, and the artistic problem. An artist, I imagine, is one who often and easily is thrown into that state of acute and sympathetic agitation which most of us, once or twice in our lives, have had the happiness of experiencing. And have you noticed that many men and most boys, when genuinely in love, find themselves, the moment the object of their emotion is withdrawn, driven by their feelings into scribbling verses ? An artist, I imagine, is always falling in love with everything. Always he is being thrown into a " state of mind." The sight of a tree or an omnibus, the screaming of whistles or the whistling of birds, the smell of roast pig, a gesture, a look, any trivial event may provoke a crisis, filling him with an intolerable desire to express himself. The artist cannot embrace the object of his emotion. He does not even wish to. Once, perhaps, that was his desire; if so, like the pointer and the setter, he has converted the barbarous pouncing instinct into the civilized pleasure of tremulous contemplation. Be that as it may, the contemplative moment is short. Simultaneously almost with the emotion arises the longing to express, to create a form that shall match the feeling, that shall commemorate the moment of ecstasy.

This moment of passionate apprehension is, unless I mistake, the source of the creative impulse; indeed, the latter seems to follow so promptly on the former that one is often tempted to regard them as a single movement. The next step is longer. The creative impulse is one thing; creation another. If the artist's form is to be the equivalent of an experience, if it is to be significant in fact, every scrap of it has got to be fused and fashioned in the white heat of his emotion. And how is his emotion to be kept at white heat through the long, cold days of formal construction? Emotions seem to grow cold and set like glue. The intense power and energy called forth by the first thrilling vision grow slack for want of incentive.

What engine is to generate the heat and make taut the energies by which alone significant form can be created ? That is where the artistic problem comes in.

The artistic problem is the problem of making a match between an emotional experience and a form that has been conceived but not created. Evidently the conception of some sort of form accompanies, or closely follows, the creative impulse. The artist says, or rather feels, to himself : I should like to express that in words, or in lines and colours, or in notes. But to make anything out of his impulse he will need something more than this vague desire to express or to create. He will need a definite, fully conceived form into which his experience can be made to fit. And this fitting, this matching of his experience with his form, will be his problem. It will serve the double purpose of concentrating his energies and stimulating his intellect. It will be at once a canal and a goad. And his energy and intellect between them will have to keep warm his emotion. Shakespeare kept tense the muscle of his mind and boiling and racing his blood by struggling to confine his turbulent spirit within the trim mould of the sonnet. Pindar, the most passionate of poets, drove and pressed his feelings through the convolutions of the ode. Bach wrote fugues. The master of St. Vitale found an equivalent for his disquieting ecstasies in severely stylistic portraits wrought in an intractable medium. Giotto expressed himself through a series of pictured legends. El Greco seems to have achieved his stupendous designs by labouring to make significant the fustian of theatrical piety.

There is apparently nothing that an artist cannot vivify. He can create a work of art out of some riddle in engineering or harmonics, an anecdote, or the frank representation of a natural object. Only, to be satisfactory, the problem must be for him who employs it a goad and a limitation. A goad that calls forth all his energies ; a limitation that focuses them on some object far more precise and comprehensible than the expression of a vague sensibility, or, to say the same thing in another way, the creation of indefinite beauty. However much an artist may have felt, he cannot just sit down and express it ; he cannot create form in the vague. He must sit down to write a play or a poem, to paint a portrait or a still life.

Almost everyone has had his moment of ecstasy, and the creative impulse is not uncommon ; but those only who have a pretty strong sense of art understand the necessity for the artistic problem. What is known of it by the public is not much liked ; it has a bad name and is reckoned unsympathetic. For the artistic problem, which limits the artist's freedom, fixes his attention on a point, and drives his emotion through narrow tubes, is what imports the conventional element into art. It seems to come between the spontaneous thrill of the artist and the receptive enthusiasm of his public with an air of artificiality. Thus, a generation brought up on Wordsworth could hardly believe in the genuineness of Racine. Our fathers and grandfathers felt, and felt rightly, that art was something that came from and spoke to the depths of the human soul. But how, said they, should deep call to deep in Alexandrines and a pseudo-classical convention, to say nothing of full-bottomed wigs ? They forgot to reckon with the artistic problem, and made the mistake that people make who fancy that nothing looking so unlike a Raphael or a Titian as a Matisse or a Picasso can be a work of art. They thought that because the stuff of art comes from the depths of human nature it can be expressed only in terms of naturalism. They did not realize that the creating of an equivalent for an æsthetic experience out of natural speech or the common forms of nature is only one amongst an infinite number of possible problems. There are still ladies who feel sure that had they been in Laura's shoes Petrarch might have experienced something more vivid than what comes through his mellifluous but elaborate *rime*. To them he would have expressed himself otherwise. Possibly : but whatever he experienced could not have become art

—significant form—till it had been withdrawn from the world of experience and converted into poetry by some such exacting problem.

One problem in itself is as good as another, just as one kind of nib is as good as another, since problems are valuable only as means. That problem is best for any particular artist that serves that particular artist best. The ideal problem will be the one that raises his power most while limiting his fancy least. The incessant recourse of European writers to dramatic form suggests that here is a problem which to them is peculiarly favourable. Its conventions, I suppose, are sufficiently strict to compel the artist to exert himself to the utmost, yet not so strict as to present those appalling technical difficulties—the sort presented by a sestina or a chant royal—that make self-expression impossible to any but a consummate master. The novel, on the other hand, as we are just beginning to suspect, affords for most writers an unsatisfactory, because insufficiently rigorous, problem. Each age has its favourites. Indeed, the history of art is very much the history of the problem. The stuff of art is always the same, and always it must be converted into form before it can become art; it is in their choice of converting-machines that the ages differ conspicuously.

Two tasks that painters and writers sometimes set themselves are often mistaken for artistic problems, but are, in fact, nothing of the sort. One is literal representation : the other the supply of genius direct from the cask. To match a realistic form with an æsthetic experience is a problem that has served well many great artists : Chardin and Tolstoi will do as examples. To make a realistic form and match it with nothing is no problem at all. Though to say just what the camera would say is beyond the skill and science of most of us, it is a task that will never raise an artist's temperature above boiling-point. A painter may go into the woods, get his thrill, go home and fetch his panel-box, and proceed to set down in cold blood what he finds before him. No good can come of it, as the gloomy walls of any official exhibition will show. Realistic novels fail for the same reason : with all their gifts, neither Zola, nor Edmond de Goncourt, nor Mr. Arnold Bennett ever produced a work of art. Also, a thorough anarchist will never be an artist, though many artists have believed that they were thorough anarchists. One man cannot pour an æsthetic experience straight into another, leaving out the problem. He cannot exude form : he must set himself to create a particular form. Automatic writing will never be poetry, nor automatic scrabbling design. The artist must submit his creative impulse to the conditions of a problem. Often great artists set their own problems ; always they are bound by them. That would be a shallow critic who supposed that Mallarmé wrote down what words he chose in what order he pleased, unbound by any sense of a definite form to be created and a most definite conception to be realized. Mallarmé was as severely bound by his problem as was Racine by his. It was as definite—for all that it was unformulated—as absolute, and as necessary. The same may be said of Picasso in his most abstract works : but not of all his followers, nor of all Mallarmé's either.

THE DOUANIER ROUSSEAU

Was he really a great painter ? A new generation is beginning to ask the question that we answered, once and for all as we thought, ten years ago. Yes, of course, the *douanier* was— a remarkable painter. The man who influenced Derain, and to some extent Picasso, is not likely to have been less. But a great painter ? For the present, at any rate, let us avoid great words.

In 1903, when first I lived in Paris, Rousseau appeared to be very much " in the movement." That was because by nature he was what thoughtful and highly trained artists were making themselves by an effort : he was direct. To us it seemed, in those days, that a mass of scientific irrelevancies and intellectual complications had come between the artist and his vision, and, again, between the vision and its expression. In a desperately practical and well-organized age, which recognized objects by their labels and never dreamed of going beneath these to discover the things themselves, artists, we thought, were in danger of losing the very stuff of which visual art is made—the direct, emotional reaction to the visible universe. People had grown so familiar with the idea of a cup, with that purely intellectual label " cup," that they never looked at a particular cup and felt its emotional significance. Also, professional painters had provided themselves with a marvellous scientific apparatus for describing " the idea of a cup " in line and colour : they had at their fingers' ends a plastic notation that corresponded with the labels by which things are intellectually recognized. They neither felt things nor expressed their feelings. For even when an artist was capable of a direct, personal reaction it was almost impossible for him not to lose it in the cogs and chains of that elaborate machinery of scientific representation to which he had been apprenticed. A determination to free artists from utilitarian vision and the disastrous science of representation was the theoretic basis of that movement which is associated with the name of Cézanne.

From the latter, at any rate, the *douanier* needed no freeing. Such science as he acquired in the course of his life was a means to expressing himself and not to picture-making. As for his vision, that was as direct and firsthand as the vision of a Primitive or a child ; and to a Primitive his admirers were in the habit of likening him, to a child his detractors. His admirers were right : his art is not childish. Primitives, because they are artists, have to grapple with the artistic problem. They have, that is, to create form that will express an emotional conception ; they have to express their sense of something they have seen and felt. A child may well have an artistic vision ;

for all that, a child is never, or hardly ever, an artist. It wrestles with no problem because it does not try to express anything. It is a mere symbolist who uses a notation not to express what it feels but to convey information. A child's drawing of a horse is not an expression of its sense of a horse, but a symbol by which other people can recognize that what occupies a certain position in its figured story is a horse. The child is not an artist, but an illustrator who uses symbolism. When, using Mr. Bertrand Russell's new symbolism, I say that $L^c 3 n 1 - C^c t =$ the Almighty, clearly I am not expressing my feeling for infinite and omnipotent goodness. Neither does the child who teases you to look at its charming coloured diagram of the farmyard expect you to share an emotional experience. Doubtless the vanity of the craftsman demands satisfaction ; but chiefly the child wishes to assure itself that some impartial judge can interpret its notation. One definitely artistic gift, however, many children do possess, and that is a sense of the decorative possibilities of their medium. This gift they have in common with the Primitives ; and this the *douanier* possessed in an extraordinary degree.

Of Rousseau's sense of the decorative possibilities of paint it is, I suppose, unnecessary to say anything. Gauguin called his black " inimitable." But, indeed, we all agree now

that, if the term " decorative " is to be used
in this limited and rather injurious sense
Rousseau, as a decorator, takes rank with the
very greatest. More important is it to realize
that Rousseau had his problem ; and that he
approached it in the spirit of a Primitive.
His reactions were as simple and genuine as
those of any child ; he experienced them with
that passion which alone provokes to creation ;
his problem was to express them sincerely and
simply in the medium of which he could make
such exquisite use. His vision was as unsophisticated as that of Orcagna, and in translating it he was as conscientious ; but he was a
smaller artist because he was less of an artist.

It has been said that Rousseau came short
of greatness for want of science. That I do
not believe. Can it be supposed that any
man who has applied himself intelligently to
any art for forty years will not have acquired
science enough to state clearly what is clear,
intense, and clamoring for expression in his
mind ? I see no reason for supposing that
Rousseau ever failed from lack of science to
express himself completely. The fault was in
what he had to express. Rousseau was in-
ferior to the great Primitives because he lacked
their taste, or, to put the matter more forcibly,
because he was less of an artist. An artist's
conception should be like a perfectly cooked
pudding—cooked all through and in every

part. His problem is to create an expressive form that shall fit exactly an artistic conception. His subject may be what he pleases. But unless that subject has been carried to the high regions of art, and there, in a dry æsthetic atmosphere, sealed up in a purely æsthetic conception it can never be externalized in pure form. That is what the great Primitives did, and what the *douanier* could not do always. In his pudding there are doughy patches. He is sentimental ; and he is not sentimental as Raphael and El Greco are.

With a race of genteel, but strangely obtuse, critics it was formerly the fashion to depreciate Raphael and El Greco on the ground that they were sentimental. Sentimental they are, in a sense. Their subjects are sentimental ; and the religiosity of some of Greco's is downright disgusting. But of these subjects every scrap has been passed through the blazing furnace of conception and fused into artistic form. It is as though a potter, working with dirty hands, had left a stain burnt by the fire into his gloriously fashioned clay. The blemish is superficial ; the form is untouched. With Rousseau it is otherwise : lumps of unfused matter break through his conception and into his design ; his pudding is not thoroughly baked. Take that well-known picture of his, *Le Présent et le Passé*, which used to be in the Jastrebzoff collection, and of which photographs are familiar to everyone : the two silly, detached heads in the sky, stuck in for sentiment's sake, are, as the saying goes, " out of the picture " and yet play the devil with it. They injure the design. What is more, in themselves they are as feeble and commonplace as the drawing of a pavement artist, which, in fact, they resemble. They are unfelt, that is the explanation—unfelt æsthetically. They have not been through the oven. They are artistically insincere. Sentimentality makes strange bedfellows. Rousseau has slipped into the very hole wherein Mr. Frank Dixie and Sir Luke Fildes disport themselves ; only, by betraying his vice in a picture that is, for the most part, so exquisitely sure in its simple, delicate expression of a frank and charming vision he gives us an impressive example of the danger, even to a good artist, of bad taste.

And there is another fault in Rousseau that springs from this lack of complete artistic integrity. He is something plebeian : he suffers a slightly self-complacent good-fellowship to creep into his pictures. Occasionally there grins through his design, and ever so little disfigures it, a touch of fatuity. He cannot help being glad that he is so simple and so good, nor quite resist telling us about it. Look at that portrait of himself—and I impose a most agreeable task, for it is charming— that portrait dated 1890, and belonging also to M. Jastrebzoff; do you not feel that the author is a little too well pleased with himself? Do you not fancy that he will soon be regaling his sitter with a good, round platitude from the exterior boulevards or a morsel from some regimental ditty in which he once excelled, that, in another moment, he will be tapping him on the back, and that he has gone a little out of his way to tell you these things? The Primitives tell us nothing of that sort; they stick to their business of creating significant form. Whatever of their personalities may reach us has passed through the transmuting fires of art: they never prattle. The Primitives are always distinguished; whereas occasionally the *douanier* is as much the reverse as the more successful painters to the British aristocracy are always.

Yet I daresay it was this jovial and unaffected good-fellowship, quite as much as his unquestionable genius, that won the brave *douanier* his place in the hearts of those brilliant people who frequented what he used to call his "soirées toutes familiales et artistiques." The artists and intellectuals of my generation —the generation that received and went down before the terrific impact of Dostoievskyism— pursued the simple and unsophisticated at least as earnestly as any follower of an earlier Rousseau. Whatever the real differences between a noble savage and an unspoilt artisan may be, the difference between the ideas of them with which a jaded society diverts itself is negligible. "Il nous faut les barbares," said Gide. Well, we have got them.* And, maybe, the next generation but one will make as much fuss about a new Matthew Arnold as we made about Marguerite Audoux.

Meanwhile the *douanier* came at the right moment. His " soirées toutes familiales et artistiques " were crowded with admirers—Picasso, Delaunay, Duhamel, Guillaume Apollinaire, Jules Romain, Max Jacob, René Arcos, Braque, André Salmon, Soffici, Blanche Albane, Marie Laurencin, elegant and eminent people from North and South America, Russia, Germany, and Scandinavia, to say nothing of his pupils (he professed both painting and music) and " les demoiselles de son quartier." The entertainment consisted, if I may trust an ear-witness, of a little bad music worse played, a little declamation, a glass of wine, and democracy untainted with the least suspicion of snobbery. There was a delicious absence of culture, on the one hand, and of romantic squalor on the other. The whole thing was solidly and sympathetically lower middle-class. The " soirée tant familiale qu'artistique " closed with a performance of the Marseillaise ; and the intelligentsia retired to bed feeling that life was full of beauty and significance.

* This essay was written a few weeks after the signing of the Armistice.

CÉZANNE*

It was the opinion of Degas that " le peintre en général est bête," and most people seem to think that Cézanne was no exception to the rule. Before agreeing, I should want to know what precisely they understood by the word " bête." Cézanne was silly certainly, but he was not stupid : he was limited and absurd, but not dull ; his opinions for the most part were conventional, but his intelligence was not common ; and his character was as obviously that of a man of genius as the most ardent hero-worshipper could desire.

Cézanne was a great character. It is a mistake to suppose that great characters are always agreeable ones. Few people, I imagine, found Cézanne agreeable ; yet painters, one would suppose, were eager to meet him that they might hear what he had to say about painting. Cézanne's ideas on painting are not like ideas at all : they are like sensations ; they have the force of sensations. They seem to give the sense of what was in his mind by a method more direct than the ordinary intellectual one. His meaning reaches us, not in a series of pellets, but in a block. These sayings of his remind one oddly of his art ; and some of his comments on life are hardly less forcible and to the point. This, for instance, provoked by

* *Paul Cézanne.* Par Ambroise Vollard. (Paris : Crès 4fr. 75.)

E

CÉZANNE

Zola's " L'Œuvre," is something more than a professional opinion :

On ne peut pas exiger d'un homme qui ne sait pas, qu'il dise des choses raisonnables sur l'art de peindre ; mais, N. de D— et Cézanne se mit à taper comme un sourd sur sa table —comment peut-il oser dire qu'un peintre se tue parce qu'il a fait un mauvais tableau ? Quand un tableau n'est pas réalisé, on le f . . . au feu, et on en recommence un autre !

Réalisé—Cézanne's incessant complaint that " he was unable to realize " has been taken by many stupid people to imply that Cézanne was conscious in himself of some peculiar and slightly humiliating inhibition from which his fellows were free ; and even M. Vollard has thought it necessary to be continually apologizing for and explaining away the phrase, which, moreover, he never does explain. Yet the explanation is as simple as can be. Genius of the very highest order never, probably, succeeds in completely realizing its conceptions, because its conceptions are unrealizable. When Cézanne envied M. Bouguereau his power of realization he was perfectly sincere and perfectly sensible. A Bouguereau can realize completely the little nasty things that are in his mind : if a Cézanne, a Shakespeare, or an Æschylus could realize as completely all that was in his the human race would think more of itself than it does. Cézanne's consciousness of the impossibility of realizing completely his conceptions—his consciousness,

rather, that he had not completely realized
them—made him regard all his pictures as un-
finished. Some day, he thought—or liked to
believe—he would push them a little further.
His habit of destroying his own works, however, had nothing to do with any sense of
failure or incapacity. It was simply a manifestation of rage and a means of appeasement.
Some people like cups and saucers : Cézanne
preferred oil-paintings, and his own were always to hand. A word of commendation for
" les professeurs " (" qui n'ont rien dans le ven
. . n . . tr . . re—les salauds—les châtrés
—les j . f . . . s ") or the least denigration
of Chardin or Delacroix was sure to cost a still-
life or a water-colour at any rate.

It is surprising that M. Vollard should not
have made this more clear, for he certainly
understood the genius and character of Cézanne.
His book is an amazingly vivid presentment of
both ; and to have made such a book out
of the life of a man whose whole life went into
the art of painting is a remarkable feat. For
Cézanne poured all his prodigious energy and
genius into a funnel that ended in the point
of his brush. He was a painter if ever there
was one, and he was nothing else ; he had no
notion of being anything else. There is
enough in Paris, one would have supposed,
to attract from himself for a moment the attention of the most preoccupied and self-absorbed

of men. When Cézanne lived in Paris he rose early, painted as long as there was light to paint by, and went to bed immediately after dinner. The time during which he was not painting he seems to have spent in wondering whether the light would be satisfactory (" gris clair ") next day. Cézanne in Paris, like the peasant in the country, spent most of his spare time thinking about the weather.

Comme il se couchait de très bonne heure, il lui arrivait de s'éveiller au milieu de la nuit. Hanté par son idée fixe, il ouvrait la fenêtre. Une fois rassuré, avant de regagner son lit il allait, une bougie à la main, revoir l'étude qui était en train. Si l'impression était bonne, il réveillait sa femme pour lui faire partager sa satisfaction. Et pour la dédommager de ce dérangement, il l'invitait à faire une partie de dames.

All of Cézanne went into his painting ; only now and then a drop escaped that voracious funnel and splashed onto life. It is by collecting and arranging these odd drops and splashes that M. Vollard has managed to construct his lively picture of this extraordinary character. It is because his task must have been so abominably exacting—the task of catching the artist outside his work—that we easily forgive him a few lapses from good sense when he is not talking about his hero. It is annoying, nevertheless, to hear quite so much of the stupid and insensitive people who attacked and insulted Cézanne. M. Vollard never tires of telling us about those who hid

their Cézannes or threw them out of window,
or sold them for next to nothing and would
now give their eyes to get them back ; of those
who jeered at Cézanne and would not hang his
pictures at exhibitions, refusing him that public
recognition he was human enough to covet—
in a word, of the now discomfited and penitent
majority. I had thoughts once of printing a
selection from the press-cuttings that reached
us at the Grafton Galleries during the first
Post-Impressionist exhibition. It would have
revealed our leading critics and experts, our
professors and directors, our connoisseurs, our
more cultivated dealers and our most popular
painters vying with each other in heaping abuse
and ridicule on the heads of Cézanne, Gauguin,
and Van Gogh. The project is abandoned.
That sort of thing I perceive becomes a bore.
And I only wish M. Vollard had perceived it
when he was writing about Zola. Zola failed
to appreciate Cézanne, of course. Zola was
an ordinary middle-class man : he was vain,
vulgar, petty ; he longed for the consideration
of people like himself, and was therefore
ostentatious ; he had a passion for money and
notoriety ; he wanted to be thought not only
clever but good ; he preached, he deprecated,
he took a moral standpoint and judged by results ; and his taste was execrable. We meet
people of Zola's sort every day in third-class
railway carriages and first, on the tops of omni-

buses and in Chelsea drawing-rooms, at the music-hall, at the opera, at classical concerts, and in Bond Street galleries. We take them for granted and are perfectly civil to them. So why, because he happened to have an astonishing gift of statement and rapid generalization, should Zola be treated as though he were a monster? Though Diggle, the billiards champion, care little or nothing for poetry, he may have an excellent heart, as well as a hand far surpassing in dexterity that of our most accomplished portrait-painters. No one dreams of reviling him.

Let us be equally just to Zola; let us notice, too, how amusingly he sets off Cézanne. Both were greatly gifted men: neither was the man of intelligence and talent, the brilliant man with the discursive intellect, who carries his gift about with him, takes it out when and where he pleases, and applies it where and how he likes. Zola, when he was not using his gift, posed as an artist, a saint, or simply "a great man"; but he never contrived to be anything but a bourgeois—a "sale bourgeois," according to Cézanne. Cézanne was all gift: seen as anything but a painter he looked like a fool. At Aix he tried to pass for a respectable *rentier*: he found no difficulty in being silly, but he could not achieve the necessary commonplaceness. He could not be vulgar. He was always an artist.

CÉZANNE

Instead of telling us so much about Zola and *tutti quanti* M. Vollard might have told us more about Cézanne's artistic development. What, for instance, is the history of his relations with Impressionism? The matter is to me far from clear. Cézanne began his artistic life amongst the Impressionists, he was reckoned a disciple of Pissarro; yet it is plain from his early work that he never swallowed much of the doctrine. Gradually he came to think that the Impressionists were on the wrong tack, that their work was flimsy and their theory misleading, that they failed to "realize." He dreamed of combining their delicate vision, their exquisite *sensation*, with a more positive and elaborate statement. He wanted to make of Impressionism "quelque chose de solide et de durable comme l'art des Musées." He succeeded. But at what moment did his dissent become acute, and to what extent was he aware from the first of its existence? Towards the end of his life he took to scolding the Impressionists, but one fancies that he was never very willing that anyone else should abuse them. "Regardez," said he to a young painter who had caught him coming out of church one stormy Sunday morning, as he pointed to a puddle touched by a sudden ray of sunlight, "comment voulez-vous rendre cela? Il faut se méfier, je vous le dis, des Impressionnistes . . . Tout de même, ils voient juste!"

CÉZANNE

The critical moment in Cézanne's life—if in such a life one moment may without impertinence be thought more critical than another—must have come somewhere about 1870. M. Vollard once asked him what he did during the war. " Ecoutez un peu, monsieur Vollard! Pendant la guerre j'ai beaucoup travaillé sur le motif à l'Estaque." M. Vollard is too good a patriot to add that during the war he also went into hiding, having been called up for military service. Cézanne, I am sorry to say, was an *insoumis*—a deserter. He seems to have supposed that he had something more important to do than to get himself killed for his country. It was not only in art that Cézanne gave proof of a surprisingly sure sense of values. Some fulsome journalist, wishing to flatter the old man after he had become famous, represented him hugging a tree and, with tears in his eyes, crying : " Comme je voudrais, celui-là, le transporter sur ma toile!" For a moment Cézanne contemplated the picture in terrified amazement, then exclaimed : " Dites, monsieur Vollard, c'est effrayant, la vie!" Useless to blame the particular imbecile : it was the world in which such things were possible that filled him with dismay. I stretch my hand towards a copy of the *Burlington Magazine* and come plumb on the following by the present Director of the Tate Gallery :

The truth is that the ecstasy of art and good actions are closely interrelated, the one leading to the other in endless succession or possibly even progression.

" Dites, monsieur Vollard, c'est effrayant, la vie ! "*

* Since writing these words I learn that the director of the Tate Gallery has been unable to find, in his series of vast rooms, space for two small and fine works by Cézanne. It is some consolation to know that he has found space for more than twenty by Professor Tonks.

RENOIR *

Renoir is the greatest painter alive.† There are admirers of Matisse and admirers of Picasso who will contradict that, though the artists themselves would probably agree. Also, there are admirers of M. Bouguereau and of Sir Marcus Stone, there are Italian Futurists and members of the New English Art Club, with whom one bandies no words. Renoir is the greatest painter alive.

He is over forty : to be exact, he is seventy-seven years old. Yet, in the teeth of modern theories that have at least the air of physiological certainties, one must admit that he is alive still. A comparison between the five-and-thirty photographs reproduced by M. Besson and those at the end of Herr Meier-Graefe's monograph suggests that even since 1910 his art has developed. But what is certain is that, during his last period, since 1900 that is to say, though so crippled by rheumatism that it is with agonizing difficulty he handles a brush, he has produced works that surpass even the masterpieces of his middle age.

Renoir was born in 1841, and in '54 bound prentice to a china-painter. A fortunate invention deprived him of this means of livelihood and drove him into oil. He escaped

* *Renoir*. Par Albert André. Crès et Cie.
† This essay was written in 1919. He died in 1920.

early from the École des Beaux-Arts, and, of course, came under the influence of Courbet. By 1863 he was being duly refused at the Salon and howled at by the respectable mob. He thus made one of the famous *Salon des Refusés*, and has, in consequence, been generally described as an " Impressionist." It is an honour he neither desires nor deserves. The pure doctrine of Impressionism, as formulated by Claude Monet, enjoins " scientific truth " and submission to Nature, whereas Renoir observed one day to an astonished disciple, " Avec la Nature on ne fait rien " ; and on being asked where, then, the student should learn his art added, without any apparent sign of shame or sense of sin—" Au musée, parbleu! "

Renoir thus affirmed what every artist knows, that art is the creation and not the imitation of form. In his eyes the most valuable part of an artist's education is the intelligent study of what other artists have done. For his own part he studied Courbet and then Delacroix, and, assuredly, from these picked up useful hints for converting sensibility into significant form. Sensibility he never lacked. Renoir's painting gift may, without unpardonable silliness, be compared with the singing gift of Mozart. His conspicuous characteristics are loveliness and ease. No painter, I suppose, gives more delight, or gives it more frankly. That is why his name provokes an odd, personal enthusiasm in thousands of people who have never seen him. That is why Frenchmen, who have sometimes a terribly intimate way of explaining themselves, have been known to assert that they feel for Renoir the sort of grateful affection that every sensitive man feels for a woman who has given him joy.

But Renoir's natural masters—parents one would say if a man could have more than two—were Fragonard, Boucher, and Watteau. These, two of whom he has surpassed, with Rubens, whom he almost equals, are responsible for most of what is derivative in his art during his first great period (1870-1881). That this should be the period beloved of amateurs does not surprise me. It is the period of *Mme. Maître* (1871), *La Loge* (1874), *Moulin de la Galette* (1876), and *M. Choquet*—" portrait d'un fou par un fou," Renoir calls it—pictures of ravishing loveliness to set dancing every chord in a spectator of normal sensibility. Also, it is a period that has an extraordinary charm for the literary connoisseur. It throws glamour over the " seventies," and, for that matter, on to the " eighties." Here are the characters of Flaubert and Maupassant as we should wish them to be. That *déjeuner* by the Seine was probably organized by the resourceful Jean de Servigny, and there, sure enough, is Yvette with a fringe. The purest of painters becomes historical by accident. He expresses the unalloyed sensibility of an artist in terms of delicious contemporary life and gives us, adventitiously, romance. A fascinating period, but not the great one.

Towards the end of 1881 Renoir set out on a tour in Italy, and, as if to show how little he was affected by what he found there, painted at Naples a large and important *Baigneuse* (now in the Durand-Ruel collection) in which I can discover not the slightest trace of Italian influence. He is too thorough a Frenchman to be much of anything else. The emphatic statement and counter-statement of the great Primitives is not in his way. He prefers to insinuate. Even in his most glorious moments he is discreet and tactful, fonder of a transition than an opposition, never passionate. The new thing that came into his art about this time, and was to affect it for the next twenty years, was not Italy but Ingres.

The influence was at first an unhappy one. During three or four years, unable, it seems, to match the new conception of form with his intensely personal reaction, Renoir produced a certain number of unconvincing and uncharacteristic pictures (*e.g.*, the dance series, *Danse à la Ville*, etc.). There is an uneasy harshness about the contours, the forms are imperfectly felt, they are wooden even, and in their placing one misses the old inevitability. Signed with another name these essays might by a dashing critic be called doctrinaire. Then in 1885 came the first *Baigneuses* (collection J. E. Blanche), whereby Renoir put himself a good head above all contemporaries save Cézanne. If this picture were hung in a public gallery, and the numerous drawings made for it ranged alongside, how finely discredited would be those knowing ones who, in their desire to emphasize the difference between form and that of which form is composed, are in the habit of calling Renoir a great colourist and then pausing impressively. I suppose it is because he rarely uses a lead pencil that the wiseacres are able to fulfil their destiny. Drawing in charcoal or pastel need not be taken seriously ; while drawing with the brush is apparently not drawing at all. That Renoir is a great draughtsman may be inferred from almost everything he has ever done. But (though that amazing *Boy with a Cat* was achieved as early as 1868) it is the work of this period—and *Les Baigneuses*, with its attendant studies, are capital examples—that makes patent his mastery and entitles him obviously to a place between Ingres and Daumier.

That it should be difficult to find a date for the beginning of Renoir's last period does not much trouble me ; but I am sorry that it is quite impossible to indicate in words its character. One can say confidently that the new conception was being elaborated between 1895 and 1900; one can suppose that its final character was to some extent imposed on the master by his growing infirmities. A painter who can hardly move arm or fingers will neither sweep nor niggle. He must paint, if he is to paint at all, in blobs and smears and patches and soft strokes ; and it is out of these that Renoir's latest works are built up. " Built up "—the expression is absurd. Rather, it is as though forms had been melted down to their component colours, and the pool of iridescent loveliness thus created fixed by a touch of the master's magic—lightly frozen over by an enchanting frost. Only ice is cold. At any rate, what happens to the spectator is that first he perceives a tangle of rather hot and apparently inharmonious tones; gradually he becomes aware of a subtle, astonishing, and unlooked-for harmony; finally, from this harmony emerge completely realized and exquisitely related forms. After which, if he has any sense of art, he remains spellbound and uncritical, and ceases to bother about how the thing was done. That, at least, is my impression of Renoir's latest style. Examples of it abound in Paris, notably M. Maurice Gangnat's collection ; and it is said that the artist intends these pictures to improve by keeping.

In his pleasant, well-written introduction

RENOIR

M. Albert André gives a portrait of Renoir that is almost too good to be true: we are encouraged to believe just what we should like to believe. It is incredibly sympathetic. Yet it is very much what we might have guessed from the pictures had we dared. And, indeed, we did dare—some of us; for, besides its purely æsthetic character, its French taste and tact, the art of Renoir has over-tones to which the literary and historical intelligence cannot choose but listen. An intimate eulogy of France by a most lovable Frenchman is what, in our lazy moods, we allow these pictures to give us. They do it charmingly. For instance, though I never saw a Renoir that could justify a district visitor in showing more of her teeth than nature had already discovered, here, unmistakably, are Parisians enjoying themselves in their own Parisian way. Here is the France of the young man's fancy and the old man's envious dreams. Here, if you please, you may smell again that friture that ate so well, one Sunday at Argenteuil, twenty years ago, in the company of a young poet who must have had genius and two models who were certainly divine. And that group with the fat, young mother suckling her baby—there is all French frankness and French tenderness and family feeling without a trace of its wonted grimness and insincerity.

RENOIR

Renoir is as French as French can be, and he knows it :

Lorsque je regarde les maîtres anciens je me fais l'effet d'un bien petit bonhomme, et pourtant je crois que de tous mes ouvrages il restera assez pour m'assurer une place dans l'école française, cette école que j'aime tant, qui est si gentille, si claire, de si bonne compagnie . . . Et pas tapageuse.

Renoir will have his place in that school, but another niche has been prepared for him amongst an even grander company. When, in 1917, *Les Parapluies* (a beautiful but not very characteristic work) was placed in the National Gallery some hundred English artists and amateurs seized the opportunity of sending the master a testimony of their admiration which, rather to their surprise and to their intense joy, apparently gave pleasure. In this they said :

Dès l'instant où votre tableau s'est trouvé installé parmi les chefs-d'œuvre des maîtres anciens, nous avons eu la joie de constater qu'un de nos contemporains avait pris place d'emblée parmi les grands maîtres de la tradition européenne

They said not a word too much.

TRADITION & MOVEMENTS

Much to its embarrassment, the National Gallery finds itself possessed of that superb picture *Les Parapluies* ; and as the director at last feels obliged to exhume those masterpieces which, for so many happy months, he and his colleagues have had, albeit in the dark, to themselves, we can now see Renoir amongst his peers. He is perfectly at home there. Renoir takes his place quite simply in the great tradition ; and when Cézanne, who is still too cheap to be within the reach of a national collection, has attained a price that guarantees respectability he, too, will be seen to fit neatly into that tradition ofwhich he is as much a part as Ingres or Poussin, Raphael or Piero della Francesca.

That Cézanne was a master, just as Poussin and Piero were, and that he, like them, is part of the tradition, is what all sensitive people know and the wiser keep to themselves. For by stating the plain fact that Renoir, Cézanne, and, for that matter, Matisse are all in the great tradition of painting one seems to suggest that the tradition is something altogether different from what most people would wish it to be. If one is right it follows that it is not simply the counter-movement to the contemporary movement ; indeed, it follows that it is not a movement at all. This is intolerable. An artist, seen as the protagonist of a movement, the exponent of a theory, and the clue to an age, has a certain interest for all active-minded people; whereas, seen merely as an artist, which is how he must be seen if he is to be seen in the tradition, he is of interest only to those who care for art. The significant characteristics of an artist, considered as the representative of a movement, are those in which he differs most from other artists; set him in the traditions and his one important characteristic is the one he shares with all—his being an artist. In the tradition a work of art loses its value as a means. We must contemplate it as an end—as a direct means to æsthetic emotion rather—or let it be. Tradition, in fact, has to do with art alone; while with movements can be mixed up history, archæology, philosophy, politics, geography, fashions, religion, and crime. So, by insisting on the fact that Matisse, Cézanne, Poussin, Piero, and Giotto are all in the tradition we insist on the fact that they are all artists. We rob them of their amusing but adscititious qualities; we make them utterly uninteresting to precisely 99.99 per cent. of our fellow-creatures; and ourselves we make unpopular.

The tradition of art begins with the first artist that ever lived, and will end with the last. Always it is being enriched or modified—never is it exhausted. The earliest artists are driven to creation by an irresistible desire to express themselves. Their over-bubbling minds supply abundance of matter; difficulties begin when they try to express it. Then it is they find themselves confronted by those terrible limitations of the human mind, and by other limitations, only less terrible, imposed by the medium in which they work. Every genuine artist—every artist, that is, with something of his own to say—is faced afresh by the problem, and must solve it for himself. Nevertheless, each one who succeeds in creating an appropriate form for his peculiar experience leaves in that form a record, and from the sum of these records is deduced something, less definite far than a code, by no means a pattern or recipe, which is yet a sign and a source of half-conscious suggestion to those that follow. No artist can escape the tradition of art except by refusing to grapple with the problem; which is how most do escape it. The academic humbug uses the old language to say nothing, the bombastic charlatan devises a new one for the same purpose; but once a man has something to express, and the passion to express it, he will find himself attacking the eternal problem and leaning on the inevitable tradition. Let anyone who doubts this mention quickly the name of some artist who owes nothing to his predecessors.

Often, however, owing either to some

change in circumstances or to his innate peculiarity, a man of uncommon force and imagination will find himself with something to say for which the traditional instrument is, or at first seems to be, inadequate. What shall he do ? Why, what Giotto did, what Masaccio did, what Ronsard and the poets of the Pléiade did, what Wordsworth did, and what Cézanne has done. All these great artists struck new veins, and to work them were obliged to overhaul the tool-chest. Of the traditional instruments some they reshaped and resharpened, some they twisted out of recognition, a few they discarded, many they retained. Above all, they travelled back along the tradition, tapping it and drawing inspiration from it, nearer to its source. Very rarely does the pioneer himself work out his seam : he leaves it to successors along with his technical discoveries. These they develop, themselves making experiments as they go forward, till of the heritage to which they succeeded they have left nothing—nothing but a fashion to be flouted by the next great original genius who shall rise. Such is the shape of a movement. A master, whose sole business it is to express himself, founds it incidentally, just as incidentally he enriches the tradition from which he borrows ; successors exploit it ; pious great-grand-nephews mummify and adore it. Movements are nothing but the stuff of which

tradition is made. At any given moment
tradition ends in the contemporary movement;
the capital works of any age are almost sure
to be capital examples of that movement;
but a hundred years later, when these are
clear-set in the tradition, the movement will
have become dust and ashes—the daily bread
of historians and archæologists.

Though lecturers still hold up the Renaissance as an example of the happy and
stagnant state of the arts in a golden age when
rebels were unknown, their pupils are aware
that Giotto, the father of Renaissance painting,
broke with the *maniera greca* at least as sharply
as Cézanne did with the nineteenth-century
convention; that in the art of the fifteenth
century we have a revolt against Giottesque
which must grievously have wounded many
pious souls; and that Raphael himself stood,
in his day, for a new movement. But distance
gives a sense of proportion. We see the art
of the Italian Renaissance whole, growing out
of Byzantine and into French. The continuity
is patent; and, what is much to my purpose,
it is Giotto and his successors rather than the
artists of the Palaeologi who seem to us to carry
on the Byzantine tradition, while the heirs of
the Renaissance are not Salvator Rosa and
Carlo Dolci, but Claude and Poussin. The
great artists stand out and join hands: the con-
tests that clashed around them, the little men

that aped them, the littler that abused, have fallen into one ruin. The odd thing is that, as often as not, the big men themselves have believed that it was the tradition, and not the stupid insensibility of their fellows, that thwarted them. They have made the mistake their enemies made infallibly : they have taken a dead movement for a live tradition. For movements die; that is one of the respects in which they differ most significantly from the tradition. The movement is a vein which is worked out; the tradition a live thing that changes, grows, and persists. The artist with a new vision comes on the tradition at its near end, and finds its implements lying in a heap mixed with the fashions of the moribund movement. He chooses; he changes; what happens next will depend a good deal on the state of public opinion. Should the artist have the luck to be born in a sensitive age and an intelligent country his innovations may be accepted without undue hubbub. In that case he will realize that artists can no more dispense with the tradition than tradition can exist without artists, and will probably come to feel an almost exaggerated reverence for the monuments of the past. But should the public be dull and brutish, and hardening the dust of dead movements into what it is pleased to call "tradition," pelt with that word the thing which above all others is to dull brutes disquieting—I mean passionate conviction—the artist, finding himself assailed in the name of tradition, will probably reply, " Damn the tradition." He will protest. And, for an artist, to become a protestant is even worse than using bad language.

Only in France, so far as I know, are the men who are working out the heritage of Cézanne allowed to be artists and expected to be nothing more. Elsewhere, the public by its uncritical attitude seems to encourage them to pose as supermen or to become rebels. Assuredly I am not advocating that slightly fatuous open-mindedness which led some Germans to seize on the movement before it was well grown and deal with it as they have dealt with so many others, collecting its artists as though they were beetles, bottling them, setting them, cataloguing them, making no mistake about them, and arranging them neatly in museums for the dust to settle on. Organized alertness of that sort is only less depressing than the smartness of those Italians who pounced so promptly on the journalistic possibilities of the movement as a means of self-advertisement. All I ask for in the public is a little more intelligence and sensibility, and a more critical attitude. Surely, by now, it should be impossible to hear what I heard only the other day—Mr. Charles Shannon being extolled, to humiliate some enterprising student, as a " traditional artist." Why, it would be as sensible to call the man who makes nest-eggs a traditional Buff Orpington ! And ought it still to be possible for a cultivated dealer, because I had refused to admire a stale old crust by some young New English painter, who, to be in the movement, had misshaped a few conventionally drawn objects and put black lines round others—for a dealer, I say, who dabbles in culture to exclaim indignantly, as one did to me not long ago, " I can't think why you don't like it : it's Post-Impressionist, isn't it ? "

If we cannot lose this habit of calling artists names, at least let us know exactly what we mean by them. By associating artists with movements and counter-movements we encourage the superstition that in art there is some important distinction besides the distinction between good art and bad. There is not. Such distinctions as can be drawn between the genuine artists of one age and another, between traditional artists and eccentrics, though serviceable to historians and archæologists, are pitfalls for critics and amateurs. To him who can help us better to appreciate works of art let us be duly grateful : to him who, from their extraneous qualities, can deduce amusing theories or pleasant fancies we will listen when we have time : but to him who would persuade us that their value can in any way depend on

some non-æsthetic quality we must be positively
rude.   Now, if we are to get rid of those misleading labels from which works of art are supposed to derive a value over and above their
æsthetic value, the first to go should be those
arch-deceivers, "traditional" and "revolutionary." Let us understand that tradition
is nothing but the essence, congealed and pre-
served for us by the masters in their works,
of innumerable movements; and that movements are mere phases of the tradition from
which they spring and in which they are
swallowed up. We shall then be armed, on
the one hand, against the solemn bore who requires us to admire his imitation of an old
master because it is in the tradition; on the
other, against the portentous "Ist," whose
parthenogenetic masterpiece we are not in a
state to relish till we have sucked down the
pseudo-philosophic bolus that embodies his
eponymous "Ism." To each we shall make
the same reply: "Be so good as to remove
your irrelevant label and we will endeavour to
judge your work on its merits."

MATISSE AND PICASSO

The names go together, as do those of Shelley and Keats or Fortnum and Mason. Even to people who seldom or never look seriously at a picture they have stood, these ten years, as symbols of modernity. They are pre-eminent; and for this there is reason. Matisse and Picasso are the two immediate heirs to Cézanne. They are in the direct line; and through one of them a great part of the younger generation comes at its share of the patrimony. To their contemporaries they owe nothing: they came into the legacy and had to make what they could of it. They are the elder brothers of the movement, a fact which the movement occasionally resents by treating them as though they were its elder sisters.

Even to each other they owe nothing. Matisse, to be sure, swept for one moment out of his course by the overwhelming significance of Picasso's early abstract work, himself made a move in that direction. But this adventure he quickly, and wisely, abandoned; the problems of Cubism could have helped him nothing to materialize his peculiar sensibility. And this sensibility—this peculiar emotional reaction to what he sees—is his great gift. No one ever felt for the visible universe just what Matisse feels; or, if one did, he could not create an equivalent. Because, in addition to this magic power of creation, Matisse has been blest with extraordinary sensibility both of reaction and touch, he is a great artist ; because he trusts to it entirely he is not what for a moment apparently he wished to be—a *chef d'école*.

Picasso, on the other hand, who never tried to be anything of the sort, is the paramount influence in modern painting—subject, of course, to the supreme influence of Cézanne. All the world over are students and young painters to whom his mere name is thrilling ; to whom Picasso is the liberator. His influence is ubiquitous : even in England it is immense. Not only those who, for all their denials—denials that spring rather from ignorance than bad faith—owe almost all they have to the inventor of Cubism, but artists who float so far out of the main stream as the Spensers and the Nashes, Mr. Lamb and Mr. John, would all have painted differently had Picasso never existed.

Picasso is a born *chef d'école.* His is one of the most inventive minds in Europe. Invention is as clearly his supreme gift as sensibility is that of Matisse. His career has been a series of discoveries, each of which he has rapidly developed. A highly original and extremely happy conception enters his head, suggested, probably, by some odd thing he has seen. Forthwith he sets himself to analyze

it and disentangle those principles that account
for its peculiar happiness. He proceeds by
experiment, applying his hypothesis in the
most unlikely places. The significant elements
of negro sculpture are found to repeat their
success in the drawing of a lemon. Before
long he has established what looks like an
infallible method for producing an effect of
which, a few months earlier, no one had so
much as dreamed. This is one reason why
Picasso is a born *chef d'école*. And this is why
of each new phase in his art the earlier examples
are apt to be the more vital and well-nourished.
At the end he is approaching that formula towards which his intellectual effort tends inevitably. It is time for a new discovery.

Meanwhile a pack of hungry followers has
been eyeing the young master as he made
clearer and ever clearer the nature of his last.
To this pack he throws hint after hint. And
still the wolves pursue. You see them in
knots and clusters all along the road he has
travelled, gnawing, tugging at some unpicked
idea. Worry! worry! worry! Here is a
crowd of old laggards still lingering and
snuffling over " the blue period." A vaster
concourse is scattered about the spot where
the nigger's head fell, and of these the strongest
have carried off scraps for themselves, which
they assimilate at leisure, lying apart ; while
round the trunk of Cubism is a veritable sea of

swaying, struggling, ravenous creatures. The howling is terrific. But Picasso himself is already far away elaborating an idea that came to him one day as he contemplated a drawing by Ingres.

And, besides being extraordinarily inventive, Picasso is what they call " an intellectual artist." Those who suppose that an intellectual artist is one who spends his time on his head mistake. Milton and Mantegna were intellectual artists : it may be doubted whether Caravaggio and Rostand were artists at all. An intellectual artist is one who feels first—a peculiar state of emotion being the point of departure for all works of art—and goes on to think. Obviously Picasso has a passionate sense of the significance of form ; also, he can stand away from his passion and consider it ; apparently in this detached mood it is that he works. In art the motive power is heat always ; some drive their engines by means of boiling emotion, others by the incandescence of intellectual passion. These go forward by intense concentration on the problem ; those swing with breathless precision from feeling to feeling. Sophocles, Masaccio, and Bach are intellectuals in this sense, while Shakespeare, Correggio, and Mozart trust their sensibility almost as a bird trusts its instinct. It never entered the head of a swallow to criticize its own methods ; and if Mozart could not write a tune wrong, that was not because he had first tested his idea at every point, but because he was Mozart. Yet no one ever thought of going to a swallow for lessons in aviation ; or, rather, Dædalus did, and we all know what came of it.

That is my point. I do not presume to judge between one method of creation and another ; I shall not judge between Matisse and Picasso ; but I do say that, as a rule, it is the intellectual artist who becomes, in spite of himself, schoolmaster to the rest. And there is a reason for this. By expressing themselves intellectual artists appeal to us æsthetically ; but, in addition, by making, or seeming to make, some statement about the nature of the artistic problem they set us thinking. We feel sure they have something to say about the very stuff of art which we, clumsily enough, can grasp intellectually. With purely æsthetic qualities the intellect can do nothing : but here, it seems, is something the brain can get hold of. Therefore we study them and they become our leaders ; which does not make them our greatest artists. Matisse may yet be a better painter than Picasso.

Be that as it may, from Matisse there is little or nothing to be learned, since Matisse relies on his peculiar sensibility to bring him through. If you want to paint like him, feel what he feels, conduct it to the tips of your fingers, thence on to your canvas, and there

you are. The counsel is not encouraging.
These airy creatures try us too high. Indeed,
it sometimes strikes me that even to appreciate
them you must have a touch of their sensibility.
A critic who is apt to be sensible was com-
plaining the other day that Matisse had only
one instrument in his orchestra. There are
orchestras in which fifty instruments sound as
one. Only it takes a musician to appreciate
them. Also, one hears the others talking about
" the pretty, tinkley stuff " of Mozart. Those
who call the art of Matisse slight must either
be insensitive or know little of it. Certainly
Matisse is capable of recording, with an exquisite gesture and not much more, just the smell
of something that looked as though it would
be good to eat. These are notes. Notes are
often slight—I make the critics a present of
that. Also of this : it takes a more intense
effort of the creative imagination to leave out
what Tchehov leaves out of his short stories
than to say what Meredith put into his long
ones.

In the Plutarchian method there was ever
a snare, and I have come near treading in it.
The difference between Matisse and Picasso
is not to be stated in those sharp antitheses that
every journalist loves. Nothing could be more
obtuse than to represent one as all feeling
and the other all thought. The art of Picasso,
as a matter of fact, is perhaps more personal

even than that of Matisse, just because his sensibility is perhaps even more curious. Look at a Cubist picture by him amongst other Cubists. Here, if anywhere, amongst these abstractions you would have supposed that there was small room for idiosyncrasy. Yet at M. Léonce Rosenberg's gallery no amateur fails to spot the Picassos. His choice of colours, the appropriateness of his most astonishing audacities, the disconcerting yet delightful perfection of his taste, the unlooked-for yet positive beauty of his harmonies make Picasso one of the most personal artists alive.

And if Picasso is anything but a dry doctrinaire, Matisse is no singing bird with one little jet of spontaneous melody. I wish his sculpture were better known in England, for it disposes finely of the ridiculous notion that Matisse is a temperament without a head. Amongst his bronze and plaster figures you will find sometimes a series consisting of several versions of the same subject, in which the original superabundant conception has been reduced to bare essentials by a process which implies the severest intellectual effort. Nothing that Matisse has done gives a stronger sense of his genius, and, at the same time, makes one so sharply aware of a brilliant intelligence and of erudition even.

Amongst the hundred differences between Matisse and Picasso perhaps, after all, there

is but one on which a critic can usefully insist.
Even about that he can say little that is definite.
Only, it does appear to be true that whereas
Matisse is a pure artist, Picasso is an artist and
something more—an involuntary preacher if
you like. Neither, of course, falls into the
habit of puffing out his pictures with literary
stuff, though Picasso has, on occasions, allowed
to filter into his art a, to me, most distasteful
dash of sentimentality. That is not the point,
however. The point is that whereas both
create without commenting on life, Picasso,
by some inexplicable quality in his statement,
does unmistakably comment on art. That is
why he, and not Matisse, is master of the
modern movement.

THE PLACE OF ART IN ART CRITICISM

The knowing ones—those, I mean, who are always invited to music after tea, and often to supper after the ballet—seem now to agree that in art significant form is the thing. You are not to suppose that, in saying this, I am trying to make out that all these distinguished, or soon to be distinguished, people have been reading my book. On the contrary, I have the solidest grounds for believing that very few of them have done that; and those that have treat me no better than they treated Hegel. For, just as an Hegelian is not so much a follower of that philosopher as an expounder, one who has an interpretation of his own, and can tell you what Hegel would have said if Hegel had been endowed by The Absolute with the power of saying anything, so of those admirable people who agree, for the moment, that significant form is what matters, no two are quite agreed as to what significant form is.

Only as to what it is not is there complete unanimity; though there is a tendency to come together on one or two positive points. It is years since I met anyone, careful of his reputation, so bold as to deny that the literary and anecdotic content of a work of visual art, however charming and lively it might be, was mere surplusage. The significance of a picture, according to the *cognoscenti*, must be implicit in its forms ; its essential quality is something which appeals directly to the sensibility of any sensitive person ; and any reference to life, to be of consequence, must be a reference to that fundamental experience which is the common heritage of mankind. Thus, those who cannot bring themselves to accept the more austere definition of the term are willing to recognize as significant certain qualities which are not purely formal. They will recognize, for instance, the tragedy of Michael Angelo, the gaiety of Fra Angelico, the lyricism of Correggio, the gravity of Poussin, and the romance of Giorgione. They recognize them as pertaining, not to the subjects chosen, but to the mind and character of the artist. Such manifestations in line and colour of personality they admit as relevant ; but they are quite clear that the gossip of Frith and the touching prattle of Sir Luke Fildes are nothing to the purpose.

And so we get a school of lenient criticism which takes account of an appeal to life, provided that appeal be to universal experience and be made by purely æsthetic means. According to this theory we can be moved æsthetically by references to universal experience implicit in certain arrangements of line and colour, always provided that such references are expressions of the artist's peculiar emotion, and not mere comments on life and history or statements of fact or opinion. These by everyone are deemed unessential. No one seriously pretends that in a picture by a Primitive of some obscure incident in the life of a minor saint there is anything of true æsthetic import which, escaping the subtlest and most sensitive artist, is revealed to the expert hagiographer : neither does anyone still believe that to appreciate Sung painting one must make oneself familiar with the later developments of Buddhist metaphysics as modified by Taoist mysticism.

Such is the prevailing critical theory. What of critical practice ? It seems to me that even our best come something short of their professions ; and when I confess that I am going to pick a quarrel with such fine exponents of their craft as the critics of *The Times* and the *Nation* readers will guess that for once I mean to take my confrères seriously. Lately we have seen a hot dispute in which, unless I mistake, both these gentlemen took a hand, raging round a figure of Christ by Mr. Epstein. For me the only interesting fact that emerged from this controversy was that, apparently, most of the disputants had not so much as heard of the greatest living sculptor—I mean Maillol, of course. Certainly, with the art of Maillol clearly in his mind, it is inconceivable that one so discriminating as the critic of the *Nation* should have said, as I think he did say, that Mr. Epstein now stands for European sculpture as

Rodin stood before him.   Not only is Maillol quite obviously superior to Mr. Epstein ; in the opinion of many he is a better artist than Rodin.

But it was not around such questions as these, vexatious, no doubt, but pertinent, that controversy raged.   The questions that eminent critics, writers, and dignitaries of divers churches discussed in public, while colonels, Socialists, and cultivated theosophical ladies wrangled over them at home, were : " Has Mr. Epstein done justice to the character of Christ ? " and, " What was His character ? " Was Christ intelligent or was He something nobler, and what has Mr. Epstein to say about it ? Was He disdainful or was He sympathetic ? Was He like Mr. Bertrand Russell or more like Mr. Gladstone ?   And did Mr. Epstein see Him with the eyes of one who knew what for ages Christ had meant to Europe, or with those of a Jew of the first century ?   Questions such as these—I will not swear to any particular one of them—were what the critics threw into the arena, and no one much blames the parsons and publicists for playing football with them.   But the critics must have known that such questions were utterly irrelevant ; that it mattered not a straw whether this statue, considered as a work of art, represented Jesus Christ or John Smith.

This the critics knew : they knew that the

appeal of a work of art is essentially permanent and universal, and they knew that hardly one word in their controversy could have meant anything to the most sensitive Chinaman alive, unless he happened to be familiar with the Christian tradition and Christian ethics. If there be no more in Mr. Epstein's figure than what the critics talked about, then, should the Christian religion ever become obsolete and half-forgotten, Mr. Epstein's figure will become quite insignificant. Most of us know next to nothing about Buddhism and Totemism, and only a little about Greek myths and Byzantine theology, yet works of art historically associated with these remain, by reason of their permanent and universal, that is to say their purely æsthetic, qualities, as moving and intelligible as on the day they left their makers' hands. About Mr. Epstein's sculpture the important thing to discover is whether, and in what degree, it possesses these permanent and universal qualities. But on that subject the critics are dumb.

An instructive parallel in literary journalism occurs to me. I have noticed lately a tendency in the intellectual underworld—for here I take leave of first-class criticism—to belittle Ibsen, with the object, apparently, of magnifying Tchekov, and always it is in the name of art that Ibsen is decried. Now, if our literary ragamuffins cared twopence about art they

would all be on their knees before Ibsen, who
is, I suppose, the finest dramatic artist since
Racine. Few things are more perfect as form,
more admirably consistent and self-supporting,
than his later plays. It was he who invented
the modern dramatic method of seizing a
situation at the point at which it can last be
seized, and from there pushing it forward with
imperturbable logic and not one divagation.
As an artist Ibsen is to a considerable extent
the master of Tchehov; but, as art is the last
thing to which an English Intellectual pays
attention, this fact has been overlooked. What
our latter-day intellectuals take an interest in
is what interested their grandmothers—morals.
They prefer Tchehov's point of view to that of
Ibsen, and so do I. They are vexed by the
teaching implicit in Ibsen's tendencious plays;
so am I. Yet when I ask myself: " Is Ibsen's
moralizing worse than anyone else's ? " I am
forced to admit that it is not. The fact is all
moralizing is tedious, and is recognized as such
by everyone the moment it becomes a little
stale. Another generation, with other ideals,
will be as much irritated by Tchehov's ill-
concealed propaganda as our generation is by
Ibsen's, and as Ibsen's was by Tennyson's.
Depend upon it : by those young people in the
next generation but one who talk loudest, wear
the worst clothes, and are most earnest about
life and least sensitive to art, Tchehov will be

voted a bore. What is more, it will be in the name of art that they will cry him down.

Every now and then we hear eloquent appeals to the appropriate authorities, praying them to add to their school of journalism a department of art criticism. I hope and believe the appropriate authorities will do no such thing. Should, however, their sense of economy be insufficient to restrain them from paying this last insult to art, they will still find me waiting for them with a practical suggestion. Any student proposing to educate himself as a critic should be compelled to devote the first years of his course to the criticism of non-representative art. Set down to criticize buildings, furniture, textiles, and ceramics, he will find himself obliged to explore the depths of his own æsthetic experience. To explain honestly and precisely why he prefers this chair to that requires, he will find, a far more intense effort of the intellect and imagination than any amount of fine writing about portraits and landscape. It will force him to take account of his purely æsthetic emotions and to discover what exactly provokes them. He will be driven into that world of minute differences and subtle reactions which is the world of art. And until he knows his way about that world he would do well to express no opinion on the merits of pictures and statues.

BONNARD *

In France, where even amateurs of painting enjoy a bit of rhetoric, for two or three days after the death of Renoir one could not be long in any of their haunts without being told either that " Renoir est mort et Matisse est le plus grand peintre de France " or that " Renoir est mort et Derain," etc.   Also, so cosmopolitan is Paris, there were those who would put in the query : " Et Picasso ? " but as no Frenchman much cares to be reminded that the man who, since Cézanne, has had the greatest effect on painting is a Spaniard, this interjection was generally ill-received.   On the other hand, those who queried : " Et Bonnard ? " got a sympathetic hearing always.

M. Léon Werth deals neither in rhetoric nor in orders of merit.   Bonnard is his theme ; and on Bonnard he has written thirty-six pages without, I think, pronouncing the name of one rival, leaving to his readers the agreeable task of putting the right heads in the way of such blows as he occasionally lets fly.   Of Bonnard he has written with a delicacy of understanding hardly to be matched in contemporary criticism. He has sketched exquisitely a temperament, and if he has not told us much about its fruits, about the pictures of Bonnard that is to say, he can always refer us to the series of reproductions at the end of the volume.

* *Bonnard.*   Par Léon Werth.   Paris : Crès. 40 fr.

What M. Werth would say to the distinction implied in my last paragraph I cannot tell ; but I am sure it is important. Certainly, behind every work of art lies a temperament, a mind ; and it is this mind that creates, that causes and conditions the forms and colours of which a picture consists ; nevertheless, what we see are forms and colours, forms and colours are what move us. Doubtless, M. Werth is right in thinking that Bonnard paints beautifully because he loves what he paints ; but what Bonnard gives us is something more significant than his feeling for cups or cats or human beings. He gives us created form with a significance of its own, to the making of which went his passion and its object, but which is something quite distinct from both. He gives us a work of art.

To consider a picture by Vuillard, whose work is often compared with that of Bonnard, might help us here. Vuillard loves what he paints, and his pictures are attractive, as often as not, chiefly because they represent lovely things. A picture by Bonnard, for all its fascinating overtones, has a life entirely of its own. It is like a flower, which is beautiful not because it represents, or reminds one of, something beautiful, but because it is beautiful. A picture by Bonnard escapes from its subject, and from its author, too. And this is all-important because it is just this independent life of its own that gives to a work of art its peculiar character and power. Unluckily, about this detached life, about a work of art considered as a work of art, there is little or nothing to be said ; so perhaps M. Werth has done well to confine himself to the task of giving his readers a taste of the quality of an artist's mind. This task was difficult enough in all conscience ; the mind of Bonnard is subtle, delicate, and creative, and it has needed subtlety, delicacy, and not a little creative power, to give us even a glimpse of it.

The first thing one gets from a picture by Bonnard is a sense of perplexed, delicious colour : tones of miraculous subtlety seem to be flowing into an enchanted pool and chasing one another there. From this pool emerge gradually forms which appear sometimes vaporous and sometimes tentative, but never vapid and never woolly. When we have realized that the pool of colour is, in fact, a design of extraordinary originality and perfect coherence our æsthetic appreciation is at its height. And not until this excitement begins to flag do we notice that the picture carries a delightful overtone—that it is witty, whimsical, fantastic.

Such epithets one uses because they are the best that language affords, hoping that they will not create a false impression. They are literary terms, and the painting of Bonnard is

never literary. Whatever, by way of over-
tone, he may reveal of himself is implicit in his
forms : symbolism and caricature are not in
his way. You may catch him murmuring to
himself, " That's a funny-looking face " ; he
will never say " That's the face of a man whom
I expect you to laugh at." If you choose to
take his *Après-Midi Bourgeoise* (which is not
reproduced here) as a sly comment on family
life you may : but anyone who goes to it for the
sort of criticism he would find in the plays of
Mr. Shaw or Mr. Barker is, I am happy to say,
doomed to disappointment. What amused
Bonnard was not the implication, social, moral,
or political, of the scene, but the scene itself
—the look of the thing. Bonnard never strays
outside the world of visual art. He finds
significance in the appearance of things and
converts it into form and colour. With the
pompous symbolism of the grand-mannerist,
or the smart symbolism of the caricaturist,
or the half-baked symbolism of the pseudo-
philosophical-futuro-dynamitard he has no
truck whatever. His ambition is not to convey, without the aid of words, certain elemen-
tary ideas, unimportant facts, or obvious senti-
ments, but to create forms that shall corres-
pond with his intimate sense of the significance
of things. The paraphernalia of symbolism are
nothing to his purpose : what he requires are
subtlety of apprehension and lightness of

touch, and these are what he has.   So M. Léon
Werth meets people who complain that " Bonnard manque de noblesse."

Bonnard is not noble.   A kitten jumping on
to the table moves him, not because he sees in
that gesture a symbol of human aspiration or of
feminine instability, the spirit of youth or the
pathos of the brute creation, nor yet because
it reminds him of pretty things, but because
the sight is charming.   He will never be appreciated by people who want something from art
that is not art.   But to those who care for the
thing itself his work is peculiarly sympathetic,
because it is so thoroughly, so unmitigatedly
that of an artist ; and therefore it does not surprise me that some of them should see in him
the appropriate successor to Renoir.   Like
Renoir, he loves life as he finds it.   He, too,
enjoys intensely those good, familiar things
that perhaps only artists can enjoy to the full—
sunshine and flowers, white tables spread beneath trees, fruits, crockery, leafage, the movements of young animals, the grace of girls
and the amplitude of fat women.   Also, he
loves intimacy.   He is profoundly French.
He reminds one sometimes of Rameau and
sometimes of Ravel, sometimes of Lafontaine
and sometimes of Laforgue.

Renoir never reminded anyone of Ravel or
Laforgue.   Renoir and Bonnard are not so
much alike after all.   In fact, both as artists

and craftsmen they are extremely different. Renoir's output was enormous ; he painted with the vast ease of a lyrical giant. His selections and decisions were instinctive and immediate. He trusted his reactions implicitly. Also, there is nothing that could possibly be called whimsical, nothing critical or self-critical, about him. Bonnard, on the other hand, must be one of the most painstaking artists alive. He comes at beauty by tortuous ways, artful devices, and elaboration. He allows his vision to dawn on you by degrees : no one ever guesses at first sight how serious, how deliberately worked out his compositions are.

There is something Chinese about him ; and he is one of those rare Europeans who have dealt in " imposed " rather than " built-up " design. Bonnard's pictures grow not as trees ; they float as water-lilies. European pictures, as a rule, spring upwards, masonry-wise, from their foundations ; the design of a picture by Bonnard, like that of many Chinese pictures and Persian textiles, seems to have been laid on the canvas as one might lay cautiously on dry grass some infinitely precious figured gauze. Assuredly, the hand that lets fall these beauties is as unlike that which, even in the throes of rheumatism, affirmed with supreme confidence the mastery of Renoir, as the easy accessibility of our last old master

is unlike this shy, fastidious spirit that M. Léon
Werth, by a brilliant stroke of sympathetic
intelligence, has contrived to catch and hold
for an instant.

DUNCAN GRANT

To-day,* when the Carfax Gallery opens its doors at No. 5 Bond Street, and invites the cultivated public to look at the paintings of Duncan Grant, that public will have a chance of discovering what has for some time been known to alert critics here and abroad—that at last we have in England a painter whom Europe may have to take seriously. Nothing of the sort has happened since the time of Constable ; so naturally one is excited.

If the public knows little of Duncan Grant the public is not to blame. During the fifteen years that he has been at work not once has he held " a one-man show," while his sendings to periodic exhibitions have been rare and unobtrusive. To be sure, there is a picture by him in the Tate Gallery. But who ever thought of going there to look for a work of art ? Besides, during the last few years the Tate, like most other places of the sort, has been given over to civil servants. Duncan Grant is a scrupulous, slow, and not particularly methodical worker. His output is small ; and no sooner is a picture finished than it is carried off by one of those watchful amateurs who seem a good deal more eager to buy than he is to sell. Apparently he cares little for fame ; so the public gets few opportunities of coming acquainted with his work.

* February 6, 1920.

DUNCAN GRANT

Duncan Grant is the best English painter alive. And how English he is! (British, I should say, for he is a Highlander.) Of course, he has been influenced by Cézanne and the modern Frenchmen. He is of the movement. Superficially his work may look exotic and odd. Odd it will certainly look to people unfamiliar with painting. But anyone who has studied and understood the Italians will see at a glance that Duncan Grant is thoroughly in the great tradition ; while he who also knows the work of Wilson, Gainsborough, Crome, Cotman, Constable, and Turner will either deny that there is such a thing as an English tradition or admit that Duncan Grant is in it. For my part, I am inclined to believe that an English pictorial tradition exists, though assuredly it is a tiny and almost imperceptible rill, to be traced as often, perhaps, through English poetry as through English painting. At all events, there are national characteristics ; and these you will find asserting themselves for good or ill in the work of our better painters.

Duncan Grant's ancestors are Piero della Francesca, Gainsborough, and the Elizabethan poets. There is something Greek about him, too ; not the archæological Greek of Germany, nor yet the Græco-Roman academicism of France, but rather that romantic, sensuous Hellenism of the English literary tradition.

It is, perhaps, most obvious in his early work, where, indeed, all the influences I have named can easily be found. Then, at the right moment, he plunged headlong into the movement, became the student of Cézanne, Matisse, Picasso, though not, curiously enough, of Bonnard, the modern artist with whose work his own has the closest affinity, and, for a year or two, suffered his personality to disappear almost beneath the heavy, fertilizing spate. He painted French exercises. He was learning. He has learnt. He can now express, not someone else's ideas, but himself, completely and with delicious ease, in the language of his age. He is a finished and highly personal modern artist.

I dare say Duncan Grant's most national characteristic is the ease with which he achieves beauty. To paint beautifully comes as naturally to him as to speak English does to me. Almost all English artists of any merit have had this gift, and most of them have turned it to sorry account. It was so pleasant to please that they tried to do nothing else, so easy to do it that they scampered and gambolled down the hill that ends in mere prettiness. From this catastrophe Duncan Grant has been saved by a gift which, amongst British painters, is far from common. He is extremely intelligent. His intellect is strong enough to keep in hand that most charming and unruly of its sister gifts, sensibility. And a painter who possesses both sensibility and the intellect to direct it is in a fair way to becoming a master.

The sensibility of English artists, whether verbal or visual, is as notorious as their sense of beauty. This becomes less surprising when we reflect that the former includes the latter. The fact is, critics, with their habitual slovenliness, apply the term " sensibility " to two different things. Sometimes they are talking about the artist's imagination, and sometimes about his use of the instrument : sometimes about his reactions, and sometimes—in the case of painters—about the tips of his fingers. It is true that both qualities owe their existence to and are conditioned by one fundamental gift —a peculiar poise—a state of feeling—which may well be described as " sensibility." But, though both are consequences of this peculiar delicacy and what I should like to call " light-triggeredness " of temperament, they are by no means identical. By " sensibility " critics may mean an artist's power of responding easily and intensely to the æsthetic significance of what he sees ; this power they might call, if they cared to be precise, " sensibility of inspiration." At other times they imply no more than sensibility of touch : in which case they mean that the contact between the artist's brush and his canvas has the quality of a thrilling caress, so that it seems almost as if the instrument that bridged the gulf between his fingers and the surface of his picture must have been as much alive as himself. " Sensibility of hand-ling " or " hand-writing " is the proper name for this. In a word, there is sensibility of the imagination and sensibility of the senses : one is receptive, the other executive. Now, Dun-can Grant's reactions before the visible uni-verse are exquisitely vivid and personal, and the quality of his paint is often as charming as a kiss. He is an artist who possesses both kinds of sensibility. These are adorable gifts ; but they are not extraordinarily rare amongst Eng-lish painters of the better sort.

In my judgement Gainsborough and Duncan Grant are the English painters who have been most splendidly endowed with sensibility of both sorts, but I could name a dozen who have been handsomely supplied. In my own time there have been four—Burne-Jones (you should look at his early work), Conder, Steer, and John, all of whom had an allowance far above the average, while in America there was Whistler. No one, I suppose, would claim for any of these, save perhaps Whistler, a place even in the second rank of artists. From which it follows clearly that something more than delicacy of reaction and touch is needed to make a man first-rate. What is needed is, of course, constructive power. An artist must be able to convert his inspiration into significant form ; for in art it is not from a word to a blow, but from a tremulous, excited vision to an orderly mental conception, and from that conception, by means of the problem and with the help of technique, to externalization in form. That is where intelligence and creative power come in. And no British painter has, as yet, combined with sure and abundant sensibility power and intelligence of a sort to do perfectly, and without fail, this desperate and exacting work. In other words, there has been no British painter of the first magnitude. But I mistake, or Gainsborough, Crome, Constable, and Duncan Grant were all born with the possibility of greatness in them.

Many British (or, to make myself safe, I will say English-speaking) painters have had enough sensibility of inspiration to make them distinguished and romantic figures. Who but feels that Wilson, Blake, Reynolds, Turner, and Rossetti were remarkable men ? Others have had that facility and exquisiteness of handling which gives us the enviable and almost inexhaustible producer of charming objects— Hogarth, Cotman, Keene, Whistler, Conder, Steer, Davies. Indeed, with the exceptions of Blake and Rossetti—two heavy-handed men of genius—and Reynolds, whose reactions were something too perfunctory, I question whether there be a man in either list who wanted much for sensibility of either sort. But what

English painter could conceive and effectively carry out a work of art ? Crome, I think, has done it ; Gainsborough and Constable at any rate came near ; and it is because Duncan Grant may be the fourth name in our list that some of us are now looking forward with considerable excitement to his exhibition.

An Englishman who is an artist can hardly help being a poet ; I neither applaud nor altogether deplore the fact, though certainly it has been the ruin of many promising painters. The doom of Englishmen is not reversed for Duncan Grant : he is a poet ; but he is a poet in the right way—in the right way, I mean, for a painter to be a poet. Certainly his vision is not purely pictorial ; and because he feels the literary significance of what he sees his conceptions are apt to be literary. But he does not impose his conceptions on his pictures ; he works his pictures out of his conceptions. Anyone who will compare them with those of Rossetti or Watts will see in a moment what I mean. In Duncan Grant there is, I agree, something that reminds one unmistakably of the Elizabethan poets, something fantastic and whimsical and at the same time intensely lyrical. I should find it hard to make my meaning clearer, yet I am conscious enough that my epithets applied to painting are anything but precise. But though they may be lyrical or fantastic or witty, these pictures never tell a story or point a moral.

My notion is that Duncan Grant often starts from some mixed motif which, as he labours to reduce it to form and colour, he cuts, chips, and knocks about till you would suppose that he must have quite whittled the alloy away. But the fact is, the very material out of which he builds is coloured in poetry. The thing he has to build is a monument of pure visual art; that is what he plans, designs, elaborates, and finally executes. Only, when he has achieved it we cannot help noticing the colour of the bricks. All notice, and some enjoy, this adscititious literary overtone. Make no mistake, however, the literary element in the art of Duncan Grant is what has been left over, not what has been added. A Blake or a Watts conceives a picture and makes of it a story; a Giorgione or a Piero di Cosimo steals the germ of a poem and by curious cultivation grows out of it a picture. In the former class you will find men who may be great figures, but can never be more than mediocre artists: Duncan Grant is of the latter. He is in the English tradition without being in the English rut. He has sensibility of inspiration, beauty of touch, and poetry; but, controlling these, he has intelligence and artistic integrity. He is extremely English; but he is more of an artist than an Englishman.

NEGRO SCULPTURE

Already the Chelsea show of African and Oceanian sculpture is sending the cultivated public to the ethnographical collections in the British Museum, just as, last autumn, the show organized in Paris by M. Paul Guillaume filled the Trocadero.* Fine ladies, young painters, and exquisite amateurs are now to be seen in those long dreary rooms that once were abandoned to missionaries, anthropologists, and colonial soldiers, enhancing their prestige by pointing out to stay-at-home cousins the relics of a civilization they helped to destroy. For my part I like the change. I congratulate the galleries and admire the visitors, though the young painters, I cannot help thinking, have been a little slow.

Negro art was discovered—its real merit was first recognized, I mean—some fifteen years ago, in Paris, by the painters there. Picasso, Derain, Matisse, and Vlaminck began picking up such pieces as they could find in old curiosity and pawn shops ; with Guillaume Apollinaire, literary apostle, following apostolically at their heels. Thus a demand was created which M. Paul Guillaume was there to meet and stimulate. But, indeed, the part played by that enterprising dealer is highly commendable ; for the Trocadero collections being, unlike the British, mediocre both in quantity

* 1919.

and quality, it was he who put the most sensitive public in Europe—a little cosmopolitan group of artists, critics, and amateurs—in the way of seeing a number of first-rate things.

Because, in the past, Negro art has been treated with absurd contempt, we are all inclined now to overpraise it; and because I mean to keep my head I shall doubtless by my best friends be called a fool. Judging from the available data—no great stock, by the way—I should say that Negro art was entitled to a place amongst the great schools, but that it was no match for the greatest. With the greatest I would compare it. I would compare it with the art of the supreme Chinese periods (from Han to Sung), with archaic Greek, with Byzantine, with Mahomedan, which, for archæological purposes, begins under the Sassanians a hundred years and more before the birth of the prophet; I would compare it with Romanesque and early Italian (from Giotto to Raffael); but I would place it below all these. On the other hand, when I consider the whole corpus of black art known to us, and compare it with Assyrian, Roman, Indian, true Gothic (not Romanesque, that is to say), or late Renaissance it seems to me that the blacks have the best of it. And, on the whole, I should be inclined to place West and Central African art at any rate on a level with Egyptian. Such sweeping classifications,

however, are not to be taken too seriously.
All I want to say is that, though the capital
achievements of the greatest schools do seem
to me to have an absolute superiority over anything Negro I have seen, yet the finest black
sculpture is so rich in artistic qualities that it is
entitled to a place beside them.

I write thinking mainly of sculpture, because it was an exhibition of sculpture that set
me off. It should be remembered, however,
that perhaps the most perfect achievements of
these savages are to be found amongst their
textiles and basket-work. Here, their exquisite taste and sense of quality and their un-
surpassed gift for filling a space are seen to
greatest advantage, while their shortcomings
lie almost hid. But it is their sculpture which,
at the moment, excites us most, and by it they
may fairly be judged. Exquisiteness of quality
is its most attractive characteristic. Touch one
of these African figures and it will remind you
of the rarest Chinese porcelain. What delicacy in the artist's sense of relief and modelling
is here implied ! What tireless industry and
paitence ! Run your hand over a limb, or a
torso, or, better still, over some wooden vessel ;
there is no flaw, no break in the continuity of
the surface ; the thing is alive from end to end.
And this extraordinary sense of quality seems
to be universal amongst them. I think I
never saw a genuine nigger object that was

vulgar—except, of course, things made quite recently under European direction. This is a delicious virtue, but it is a precarious one. It is precarious because it is not self-conscious : because it has not been reached by the intelligent understanding of an artist, but springs from the instinctive taste of primitive people. I have seen an Oxfordshire labourer work himself beautifully a handle for his hoe, in the true spirit of a savage and an artist, admiring and envying all the time the lifeless machine-made article hanging, out of his reach, in the village shop. The savage gift is precarious because it is unconscious. Once let the black or the peasant become acquainted with the showy utensils of industrialism, or with cheap, realistic painting and sculpture, and, having no critical sense wherewith to protect himself, he will be bowled over for a certainty. He will admire ; he will imitate ; he will be undone.

At the root of this lack of artistic self-consciousness lies the defect which accounts for the essential inferiority of Negro to the very greatest art. Savages lack self-consciousness and the critical sense because they lack intelligence. And because they lack intelligence they are incapable of profound conceptions. Beauty, taste, quality, and skill, all are here ; but profundity of vision is not. And because they cannot grasp complicated ideas they fail generally to create organic wholes. One of the chief characteristics of the very greatest artists is this power of creating wholes which, as wholes, are of infinitely greater value than the sum of their parts. That, it seems to me, is what savage artists generally fail to do.

Also, they lack originality. I do not forget that Negro sculptors have had to work in a very strict convention. They have been making figures of tribal gods and fetiches, and have been obliged meticulously to respect the tradition. But were not European Primitives and Buddhists similarly bound, and did they not contrive to circumvent their doctrinal limitations ? That the African artists seem hardly to have attempted to conceive the figure afresh for themselves and realize in wood a personal vision does, I think, imply a definite want of creative imagination. Just how serious a defect you will hold this to be will depend on the degree of importance you attach to complete self-expression. Savage artists seem to express themselves in details. You must seek their personality in the quality of their relief, their modulation of surface, their handling of material, and their choice of ornament. Seek, and you will be handsomely rewarded ; in these things the niggers have never been surpassed. Only when you begin to look for that passionate affirmation of a personal vision

which we Europeans, at any rate, expect to
find in the greatest art will you run a risk
of being disappointed. It will be then, if ever,
that you will be tempted to think that these
exquisitely gifted black artists are perhaps as
much like birds building their nests as men
expressing their profoundest emotions.

And now come the inevitable questions—
where were these things made, and when ?
" At different times and in different places,"
would be the most sensible reply. About
the provenance of any particular piece it is
generally possible to say something vague ;
about dates we know next to nothing. At least,
I do ; and when I consider that we have no
records and no trustworthy criteria, and that
so learned and brilliant an archæologist as Mr.
Joyce professes ignorance, I am not much disposed to believe that anyone knows more.
I am aware that certain amateurs think to en-
hance the value of their collections by confer-
ring dates on their choicer specimens ; I can
understand why dealers encourage them in this
vanity ; and, seeing that they go to the col-
lectors and dealers for their information, I
suppose one ought not to be surprised when
journalists come out with their astounding
attributions. The facts are as follows.

We know that Portuguese adventurers had a
considerable influence on African art in the
sixteenth, and even in the fifteenth, century.

There begins our certain knowledge. Of work so influenced a small quantity exists. Of earlier periods we know nothing precise. There are oral traditions of migrations, empires, and dynasties : often there is evidence of past invasions and the supersession of one culture by another : and that is all. The discoveries of explorers have so far thrown little light on archæology ; and in most parts of West and Central Africa it would be impossible even for trained archæologists to establish a chronological sequence such as can be formed when objects are found buried in the sand one above the other. But, in fact, it is to vague traders and missionaries, rather than to trained archæologists, that we owe most of our fine pieces, which, as often as not, have been passed from hand to hand till, after many wanderings, they reached the coast. Add to all this the fact that most African sculpture is in wood (except, of course, those famous products of early European influence, the bronze castings from Benin), that this wood is exposed to a devastating climate—hot and damp—to say nothing of the still more deadly white ants, and you will probably agree that the dealer or amateur who betickets his prizes with such little tags as "Gaboon, 10th century" evinces a perhaps exaggerated confidence in our gullibility.

Whenever these artists may have flourished

it seems they flourish no more. The production of idols and fetiches continues, but the
production of fine art is apparently at an end.
The tradition is moribund, a misfortune one
is tempted to attribute, along with most that
have lately afflicted that unhappy continent,
to the whites. To do so, however, would not
be altogether just. Such evidence as we possess—and pretty slight it is—goes to show
that even in the uninvaded parts of West
Central Africa the arts are decadent : wherever
the modern white man has been busy they are,
of course, extinct. According to experts Negro
art already in the eighteenth century was
falling into a decline from some obscure, inter-
nal cause. Be that as it may, it was doomed
in any case. Before the bagman with his
Brummagem goods an art of this sort was
bound to go the way that in Europe our applied
arts, the art of the potter, the weaver, the builder
and the joiner, the arts that in some sort resembled it, have gone. No purely instinctive
art can stand against the machine. And thus
it comes about that, at the present moment,
we have in Europe the extraordinary spectacle
of a grand efflorescence of the highly self-
conscious, self-critical, intellectual, individualistic art of painting amongst the ruins of the
instinctive, uncritical, communal, and easily
impressed arts of utility. Industrialism, which,
with its vulgar finish and superabundant orna-

ment, has destroyed not only popular art but popular taste, has merely isolated the self-conscious artist and the critical appreciator; and the nineteenth century (from Stephenson to Mr. Ford), which ruined the crafts, in painting (from Ingres to Picasso) rivals the fifteenth.

Meanwhile, the scholarly activities of dealers and journalists notwithstanding, there is no such thing as nigger archæology; for which let us be thankful. Here, at any rate, are no great names to scare us into dishonest admiration. Here is no question of dates and schools to give the lecturer his chance of spoiling our pleasure. Here is nothing to distract our attention from the one thing that matters—æsthetic significance. Here is nigger sculpture: you may like it or dislike it, but at any rate you have no inducement to judge it on anything but its merits.

I

ORDER AND AUTHORITY

I

M. André Lhote is not only a first-rate painter, he is a capable writer as well ; so when, some weeks ago, he began to tell us what was wrong with modern art, and how to put it right, naturally we pricked up our ears. We were not disappointed. M. Lhote had several good things to say, and he said them clearly ; the thing, however, which he said most emphatically of all was that he, André Lhote, besides being a painter and a writer, is a Frenchman. He has a natural taste for order and a superstitious belief in authority. That is why he recommends to the reverent study of the young of all nations, David—David the Schoolmaster ! *Merci*, we have our own Professor Tonks.

Not that I would compare David, who was a first-rate practitioner and something of an artist, with the great Agrippa of the Slade. But from David even we have little or nothing to learn. For one thing, art cannot be taught ; for another, if it could be, a dry doctrinaire is not the man to teach it. Very justly M. Lhote compares the Bouchers and Fragonards of the eighteenth century with the Impressionists : alike they were charming, a little drunk and disorderly. But when he asserts that it was David who rescued painting from their agreeable frivolity he must be prepared for contradiction : some people will have it that it was rather the pupil Ingres. David, they will say, was little better than a politic pedagogue, who, observing that with the Revolution classical virtues and classical costumes had come into fashion, that Brutus, the tyrannicide, and Aristides, called "the just," were the heroes of the hour, suited his manners to his company and gave the public an art worthy of highly self-conscious liberals. The timely discoveries made at Herculaneum and Pompeii, they will argue, stood him in good stead. From these he learnt just how citizens and citizen-soldiers should be drawn ; and he drew them : with the result that the next generation of Frenchmen were sighing,

> Qui nous délivrera des Grecs et des Romains ?

Whoever may have rescued European painting from the charming disorder of the age of reason, there can be no question as to who saved it from the riot of impressionism. That was the doing of the Post-Impressionists headed by Cézanne. Forms and colours must be so organized as to compose coherent and self-supporting wholes ; that is the central conviction which has inspired the art of the last twenty years. Order : that has been the watchword ; but order imposed from within. And order so imposed, order imposed by the artist's inmost sense of what a work of art should be, is something altogether different from the order obtained by submission to a theory of painting. One springs from a personal conviction ; the other is enjoined by authority. Modern artists tend to feel strongly the necessity for the former, and, if they be Frenchmen, to believe intellectually in the propriety of the latter.

Look at a picture by Cézanne or by Picasso. What could be more orderly ? Cubism is nothing but the extreme manifestation of this passion for order, for the complete organization of forms and colours. The artist has subordinated his predilections and prejudices, his peculiar way of seeing and feeling, his whims, his fancies and his eccentricities, to a dominant sense of design. Yet the picture is personal. In the first place a picture must be an organic whole, but that whole may be made up of anything that happens to possess the artist's mind. Now, look at a picture by Baudry or Poynter and you will see the last word in painting by precept. The virtuous apprentice has stuck to the rules. He has done all that his teacher bade him do. And he has done nothing else. David ought to be pleased. Pray, M. Lhote, give him top marks.

Post-Impressionism, which reaffirmed the artist's latent sense of order and reawoke a passion to create objects complete in themselves, left the painter in full possession of his individuality. Now individualism is the breath of every artist's life, and a thing of which no

Frenchman, in his heart, can quite approve. So, if an artist happens also to be a Frenchman —and the combination is admirably common— what is he to do? Why, look one way and row the other; which is what M. Lhote does. He paints delightfully personal and impenitent pictures, and preaches artistic Cæsarism and David, " the saviour of society." All the week he is a French artist, traditional as all real artists must be, but never denying, when it comes to practice, that tradition is merely an indispensable means to self-expression; and on Sundays, I dare say, he goes, like Cézanne, to lean on M. le Curé, who leans on Rome, while his *concierge* receives the pure gospel of Syndicalism, which, also, is based on absolute truths, immutable, and above criticism.

It is notorious that you may with impunity call a placable Frenchman " butor," " scélérat," " coquin fieffé," " sale chameau," " député " even, or " sénateur "; but two things you may not do: you may not call him " espèce d'individu," and you may not say " vous n'êtes pas logique." It is as unpardonable to call a Frenchman " illogique " as to shout after the Venetian who has almost capsized your gondola " mal educato." M. Lhote is " logique " all right: but " logical " in France has a peculiar meaning. It means that you accept the consequences of your generalizations without bothering about any little discrepancies

that may occur between those consequences
and the facts ascertained by experience; it
does not mean that your high *a priori* generalizations are themselves to be tested by the nasty,
searching instrument of reason. Thus it
comes about that the second master to whom
M. Lhote would put this wild and wilful age
of ours to school is that mysterious trinity of
painters which goes by the name of " Le
Nain."

I can quite understand M. Lhote's liking
for the brothers Le Nain, because I share it.
Their simple, honest vision and frank statement are peculiarly sympathetic to the generation that swears by Cézanne. Here are men
of good faith who feel things directly, and say
not a word more than they feel. With a little
ingenuity and disingenuousness one might
make a *douanier* of them. They are scrupulous, sincere, and born painters. But they are
not orderly. They are not organizers of form
and colour. No: they are not. On the contrary, these good fellows had the most ele-
mentary notions of composition. They seem
hardly to have guessed that what one sees is
but a transitory and incoherent fragment out
of which it is the business of art to draw per-
manence and unity. They set down what they
saw, and it is a bit of good luck if what they
saw turns out to have somewhat the air of a
whole. Yet M. Lhote, preaching his crusade

against disorder, picks out the Le Nain and
sets them up as an example. What is the
meaning of this?

M. Lhote himself supplies the answer. It
is not order so much as authority that he is
after; and authority is good wherever found
and by whomsoever exercised. "Look," says
he, "at Le Nain's peasants. The painter represents them to us in the most ordinary attitude. It is the poetry of everyday duties
accepted without revolt. Le Nain's person-
ages are engaged in being independent as
little as possible." No Bolshevism here: and
what a lesson for us all! Let painters submit
themselves lowly and reverently to David, and
seventeenth-century peasants to their feudal
superiors. Not that I have the least reason
for supposing M. Lhote to be in politics an
aristocrat: probably he is a better democrat
than I am. It is the κράτος, the rule, he cares
for. Do as you are told by Louis XIV, or
Lenin, or David: only be sure that it is as
you are told. M. Lhote, of course, does nothing of the sort. He respects the tradition,
he takes tips from Watteau or Ingres or
Cézanne, but orders he takes from no man.
He is an artist, you see.

In many ways this respect for authority has
served French art well. It is the source of
that traditionalism, that tradition of high
seriousness, craftsmanship, and good taste,

which, even in the darkest days of early Victorianism, saved French painting from falling into the pit of stale vulgarity out of which English has hardly yet crawled. French revolutions in painting are fruitful, English barren —let the Pre-Raphaelite movement be my witness. The harvest sown by Turner and Constable was garnered abroad. Revolutions depart from tradition. Yes, but they depart as a tree departs from the earth. They grow out of it ; and in England there is no soil. On the other hand, it is French conventionality —for that is what this taste for discipline comes to—which holds down French painting, as a whole, below Italian. There are journeys a Frenchman dare not take because, before he reached their end, he would be confronted by one of those bogeys before which the stoutest French heart quails—" C'est inadmissible," " C'est convenu," " La patrie en danger." One day he may be called upon to break bounds, to renounce the national tradition, deny the pre-eminence of his country, question the sufficiency of Poussin and the perfection of Racine, or conceive it possible that some person or thing should be more noble, reverend, and touching than his mother. On that day the Frenchman will turn back. " C'est inadmissible."

France, the greatest country on earth, is singularly poor in the greatest characters— great ones she has galore. Her standard of civilization, of intellectual and spiritual activity, is higher than that of any other nation ; yet an absence of vast, outstanding figures is one of the most obvious facts in her history. Her literature is to English what her painting is to Italian. Her genius is enterprising without being particularly bold or original, and though it has brought so much to perfection it has discovered comparatively little. Assuredly France is the intellectual capital of the world, since, compared with hers, all other post-Renaissance civilizations have an air distinctly provincial. Yet, face to face with the rest of the world, France is provincial herself. Here is a puzzle : a solution of which, if it is to be attempted at all, must be attempted in another chapter.

II

For the last sixty years and more one of the rare pleasures of political philosophers has been to expatiate on " le droit administratif," on the extraordinary powers enjoyed by Government in France, whatever that government may be ; and another pleasure, which few have denied themselves, is that of drawing the not very obscure inference that France is democratic rather than liberal, and that the French genius has no patience with extreme individualism. If its effects were confined wholly to politics, to criticize this national characteristic would be no part of my business ; but as it has profoundly influenced French art as well as French life and thought, the reader, I trust, will not be unbearably vexed by an essay which has little immediately to do with the subject on which I am paid to write. "What is the cause of French conventionality ? " "What are its consequences ? " These are questions to which the student of French art cannot well be indifferent ; and these are the questions that I shall attempt to answer.

The cause, I suspect, is to be found in the defect of a virtue. If it takes two to make a quarrel it takes as many to make a bargain ; and if even the best Frenchmen are willing to make terms with society, that must be because society has something to offer them worth accepting. All conventions are limitations on thought, feeling, and action ; and, as such, are the enemies of originality and character—hateful, therefore, to men richly endowed with either. French conventions, however, have a specious air of liberality, and France offers to him who will be bound by them partnership in the most perfect of modern civilizations—a civilization, be it noted, of which her conventions are themselves an expression. The bribe is tempting. Also, the pill itself is pleasantly coated. Feel thus, think thus, act thus, says the French tradition, not for moral, still less for utilitarian, reasons, but for æsthetic. Stick to the rules, not because they are right or profitable, but because they are seemly—nay, beautiful We are not telling you to be respectable, we are inviting you not to be a lout. We are offering you, free of charge, a trade mark that carries credit all the world over. " How French he (or she) is ! " Many a foreigner would pay handsomely to have as much said of him.

Any English boy born with fine sensibility, a peculiar feeling for art, or an absolutely first-rate intelligence finds himself, from the outset, at loggerheads with the world in which he is to live. For him there can be no question of accepting those conventions which express what is meanest in an unsympathetic society. To begin with, he will not go to church or chapel on Sundays : it might be different were it a question of going to Mass. The hearty conventions of family life which make impossible almost relations at all intimate or subtle arouse in him nothing but a longing for escape. He will be reared, probably, in an atmosphere where all thought that leads to no practical end is despised, or gets, at most, a perfunctory compliment when some great man who in the teeth of opposition has won to a European reputation is duly rewarded with a title or an obituary column in *The Times*. As for artists, they, unless they happen to have achieved commercial success or canonization

in some public gallery, are pretty sure to be
family jokes. Thus, all his finer feelings will
be constantly outraged; and he will live, a
truculent, shame-faced misfit, with *John Bull*
under his nose and *Punch* round the corner,
till, at some public school, a course of compulsory games and the Arnold tradition either
breaks his spirit or makes him a rebel for life.

In violent opposition to most of what sur-
rounds him, any greatly gifted, and tough,
English youth is likely to become more and
more aware of himself and his own isolation.
While his French compeer is having rough
corners gently obliterated by contact with a
well-oiled whetstone, and is growing daily
more conscious of solidarity with his partners
in a peculiar and gracious civilization, the
English lad grows steadily more individualistic.
Daily he becomes more eccentric, more ad-
venturous, and more of a " character." Very
easily will he snap all conventional cables and,
learning to rely entirely on himself, trust only
to his own sense of what is good and true and
beautiful. This personal sense is all that he
has to follow; and in following it he will meet
with no conventional obstacle that he need
hesitate for one moment to demolish. English
civilization is so smug and hypocritical, so
grossly philistine, and at bottom so brutal, that
every first-rate Englishman necessarily becomes an outlaw. He grows by kicking;

and his personality flourishes, unhampered by sympathetic, clinging conventions, nor much— and this is important, too—by the inquisitorial tyranny of Government. For, at any rate until the beginning of the war, an Englishman who dared to defy the conventions had less than a Frenchman to fear from the laws.

I have already suggested that the consequences of this difference between French and English civilization may be studied in the history of their literature and thought. For the abject poverty of English visual art I have attempted to give reasons elsewhere : here I have not space to say more than that it is rarely good for an artist to be a protestant, and that a protestant is just what the English attitude to painting generally forces a genuine artist to be. But consider the literature of the French Renaissance : Rabelais is the one vast figure. Ronsard and his friends are charming, elegant, and erudite ; but not of the stupendous. What is even more to the point, already with the *pléiade* we have a school—a school with its laws and conventions, its " thus far and no further." Nothing is more notorious than the gorgeous individualism and personality of those flamboyant monsters whom we call the Elizabethans, unless it be the absence of that quality in the great French writers of the next age. Had Pascal been as bold as Newton he might have been as big. No one will deny that

Descartes was a finer intelligence than Hobbes, or that his meticulous respect for French susceptibilities gave an altogether improbable turn to his speculations. In the eighteenth century it was the English who did the discovering and the French who, on these discoveries being declared *admissibles*, brought them to perfection. Even in the nineteenth, the Revolution notwithstanding, French genius, except in painting, asserted itself less vividly and variously than the Russian or English, and less emphatically than the German.

In recording the consequences of this French taste for authority we have had to register profit and loss. It is true that the picture presented by French history offers comparatively few colossal achievements or stupendous characters. With the latter, indeed, it is particularly ill-supplied. Whereas most of the great and many of the secondary English writers, thinkers, and artists have been great " characters," the slightly monotonous good sense and refinement of French literary and artistic life is broken only by a few such massive or surprising figures as those of Rabelais, La Fontaine, Poussin, Rousseau, Flaubert, Cézanne—a formidable list but a short one, to which, however, a few names could be added. On the other hand, what France has lost in colour she has gained in fertility ; and in a universal Honours List for intellectual and artistic prowess the number of French names would be out of all proportion to the size and wealth of the country. Furthermore, it is this traditional basis that has kept French culture up to a certain level of excellence. France has never been without standards. Therefore it has been to France that the rest of Europe has always looked for some measure of fine thinking, delicate feeling, and general amenity. Without her conventionality it may be doubted whether France could have remained so long the centre of civilization.

One commonly deplored consequence of French conventionality is that it makes Frenchmen incapable of well understanding or appreciating anything foreign, or of judging acutely between foreigners and themselves. But is even this a serious misfortune ? French critics can discriminate between French productions with unsurpassable delicacy and precision. As for the spring of French inspiration, it is so copious that the creative genius of that favoured race seems to need nothing more from outside than an occasional new point of departure, to the grasping of which its imperfect knowledge and unprehensile taste are adequate. Indeed, the rare endeavours of Frenchmen seriously to cultivate alien methods and points of view more often than not end in disaster. Shortly before the war a school of particularly intelligent and open-minded writers discovered, what we in England are only too familiar with, the æsthetic possibilities of charity and the beauty of being good. Dostoevsky began it. First, they ran after *him*; then, setting themselves, as well as they could, to study Wordsworth and Walt Whitman, in translations, they soon plunged miserably into a morass of sentimentality. A gifted novelist and a charming poet, Charles-Louis Philippe and Vildrac, were amongst the first to fall in. A Wordsworth can moralize, a Sterne can pipe his eye, with impunity; but late eighteenth- and early twentieth-century literature prove how dangerous it is for a French author to trespass in pursuit of motives beyond the limits of his tradition.

The reason why Frenchmen are incompetent to judge or appreciate what is not French is that they apply to all things the French measure. They have no universal standards, and, what is worse, they take for such their own conventions. To read a French critic on Shakespeare or Ibsen or Dostoevsky or Goethe is generally a humiliating experience for one who loves France. As often as not you will find that he is depending on a translation. It seems never to strike him that there is something ludicrous in appraising nicely the qualities of a work written in a language one cannot understand. Rather it seems to him ludicrous that books should be written in any language but his own;

and, until they are translated, for him they do not exist. Many years ago, at Cambridge, I remember having a sharpish altercation with Rupert Brooke, who had taken it upon himself to denigrate the art of Racine. Before long it came out that he had read the plays only in a translation; for at that time—he was in his second year, I think—he had little or no French. Everyone laughed, and the argument collapsed. Set the scene in Paris, imagine a detractor of Shakespeare or Goethe being convicted of similar ignorance, and ask yourself whether one Frenchman of the party would have felt that by such an admission the critic was put out of court.

It cannot be denied, I fear, that the conventional habits of the French mind lead easily to ignorance and self-satisfaction. To be frank, the complacent aberrations of French taste, with its passion for Poe and its pathetic confidence in Kipling and Chesterton, have become a standing joke abroad. There is no great reason why the French should know anything of foreign thought and literature; but there is every reason why, knowing nothing, they should refrain from comment. And how many Frenchmen do know anything? When I reflect that hardly one can quote a line of English without committing or, at any rate, permitting the grossest and most nonsensical blunders, I am inclined to suspect that the answer is, very few. And I suppose it is this combination of ignorance with an incapacity for handling criteria of universal validity which gives to the nation that is assuredly the centre of civilization its paradoxical air of provinciality. A Frenchman discoursing on foreign peoples or on mankind in general—a favourite topic— suggests to me sometimes the fantastic vision of a dog-fancier criticizing a steer. Grant his premises—that whatever he admires in the one must be essential to the other—and nothing could be more just and luminous than his remarks. Undeniably the creature is a bit thick in the girth and, what is worse, bull-necked. Only, as the points of an ox are different from those of a poodle, the criticism is something beside the mark : and there is not much more virtue in the objection to Shakespeare's later tragedies that they are not written in rhymed verse. Blank verse, however, is not in the great tradition ; and the French critic, with one eye fixed submissively on authority, doubts whether he would be justified in admiring it unreservedly. Such are the inevitable consequences of conventionality : and French conventionality is, in its turn, the inevitable consequence of a civilization so gracious and attractive that even the most lawless of its children cannot bear to appear disloyal.

MARQUET *

The best picture by Marquet I ever saw was
in the Grafton Gallery exhibition of 1912.
It represented a naked woman sitting in a rock-
ing-chair.   Since then I have seen scores of
things by him, admirable, as a rule, and in-
variably brilliant, but never one that was quite
first-rate.   And here comes M. George Besson,
with an essay and an album of photographs, to
show us a few works which, surpassing anything of which we had supposed him capable,
emerge triumphantly from that stream of clever
variations on a theme which Marquet has made
only too much his own.

Anyone who compares these nudes with what
Matisse was doing a dozen or fifteen years ago
will not fail to discover a common factor :
neither will he be surprised to learn that at one
time these two artists were treated almost as
equals.   Both achieved a strange and disquieting intensity by bold simplifications and distortion, by concentration on the vital movements and characteristics of the human body,
and by an absolute indifference to its literary
and sentimental interest.   " Lorsque je dessine
j'ai devant un homme les mêmes préoccupa-
tions que devant un bec de gaz."   That is well
said : what is more, the saying has been put
successfully into practice.   Such pictures as
numbers 19, 25, and 27 are entitled to a

* *Marquet.*   Par George Besson.

place beside those of no matter what contemporary.

Needless to say, the integrity of Marquet's vision has considerably distressed those who have no taste for art ; and from one of them, Marquet's friend Charles-Louis Philippe, it drew a bit of art criticism that ought not to be lost. " Le ciel me préserve," exclaims the author of *Marie Donadieu*, " d'aimer d'un amour total un art dont l'ironie parfois atteint à la cruauté ! Et quand, tous les usages admis qui veulent qu'on ne présente un homme que sous ses bons côtés, quand l'amitié même que j'éprouve pour M. Marquet, m'eussent engagé, à me taire, un devoir plus impérieux me sollicitait, et j'aurais eu le sentiment de me rabaisser moi-même en y manquant."

Not even an art critic can be expected to lower himself in his own eyes by turning a deaf ear to the solicitations of imperious duty. So Monsieur Philippe very honourably concludes his observations by expressing the opinion that " il n'a pas droit à toute l'admiration des hommes puisqu'il a été sans pitié."

The cry of this soft and silly sentimentalist has been neatly put by M. Besson to the purpose of illustrating, and perhaps a little exaggerating, the merits of a painter who is, assuredly, neither one nor the other. Too clever by half, that rather is the fault with which Marquet must be taxed. The artist who has

given us a dozen first-rate things—superb
nudes, "felt" as solid, three-dimensional
forms, and realized as such—is always being
forestalled by an astonishing caricaturist who
can knock you off something brilliant, rapid,
and telling while you wait for the boat. Always this brisk and agile person is stepping
forward in front of the artist and jotting down
his neat symbols in the space reserved for
significant form. The landscapes and boats
and street-scenes of Marquet, with their
joyously emphatic statement, their lively con-
trasts, and their power of giving you the pith
of the matter in a few strokes, are about as
valuable as the best things of Forain. They
are statements of fact, not expressions of
emotion. Marquet, the inimitable captor of
life as it hurries by, is not much better than a
caricaturist ; and as he becomes more and more
proficient in his craft he bothers less and less
about that to which it should be a means.
The art of Marquet tends ever to become the
repetition of a formula.

Lately, in London, we have been looking at
the works of Pissarro, and I could wish that
Marquet would look at them, too. Like him,
Pissarro was a painter of streets and landscapes
who returned again and again to the same
motif. In the course of a long life he must,
I should think, have painted the Quai Voltaire,
the Quai des Grands Augustins, and the Quai

St. Michel almost as often as Marquet has knocked them off. And if Pissarro never invented a shorthand wherewith to make notes of what was going on beneath his window, that was because Pissarro, for all his impressionist theory, was less concerned with the transitory aspect of things than with their æsthetic significance. He, too, approached everything, men and women, trees, rivers, and houses, in the same spirit : he approached them in the spirit of a painter. Never for the ugliest harlot, the sorriest thief, or the most woe-begone gas-jet did he feel that whimpering, simpering, sentiment that Tolstoy frankly admired and Philippe felt the want of. But always he seems to have seen his motif with the finely disinterested passion of an artist. Now, the passion of an artist is not to be jotted down : it has to be deliberately transmuted into form.

If Marquet were as familiar with naked women as he is with the hats, coats, and petti-coats he sees from his window, doubtless by this time he would have elaborated a set of symbols wherewith to record his sense of them. Happily he is not : so, before the model, he finds himself obliged to demand of the artist that is in him some plastic equivalent for his intense and agitated vision. Thus goaded and disarmed he can produce a masterpiece. And, therefore, were it for me to give advice, what I should say to Marquet would be—throw away

your sketch-book and panel-box, and settle
down in a studio, with a top light, a model or
two, and a six-foot canvas. Only, as this must
be just what M. Lhote has been telling him,
naturally he would tell me to mind my own
business.

His apologist, M. Besson, at any rate, has no
patience with those who would set artists in the
way they should go. In this essay he gives
them a piece of his mind, and he does it so well
and so gaily that it is a pleasure to be scolded.
First, he has a few words with " une dame, que
Gérome fit héritière de ses uniformes et qui
devint la muse d'un géomètre-arpenteur de
certaine récente peinture." (Whom can he
mean ?)

Je connais l'atelier de Marquet, Madame, en marge de
l'Atelier où l'on esthétise, où l'on fabrique les manifestes et
les novateurs de génie. Marquet garde son rôle de peintre.
Il n'est guère pour lui de souci plus sérieux que le souci de
sa liberté. Il veut être libre pour peindre, libre même pour
oublier la peinture, libre encore, libre davantage pour n'être
ni questionné ni consulté, pour ne devenir ni un expert, ni
un éducateur de sots.

Et voilà pourquoi, vous n'avez jamais fait de conférence
en son atelier.

And again :

Pour n'avoir jamais asservi son art à la construction d'un
système, pour avoir senti la vanité des théories, pour n'avoir
pas fait tout les pèlerinages d'où l'on revient avec des règles,
l'art d'Albert Marquet donne une impression de peinture
heureuse.

Of course M. Besson is right. Few in this world cut a more ludicrous figure than art-masters ; few things are more deplorable than propaganda. Yet M. Besson should be careful : one thing there is more ridiculous still, and that is counter-propaganda. Protestantism in art is the devil ; but the devil is not such a fool as to protest against protestantism. He leaves that to the young bloods of the Rotonde and the Café Royal. By all means let M. Besson claim liberty for his artist, but, in doing so, let him beware of denying it to another, even though what that other demands be " liberty of prophesying " or the right to preach the gospel according to David.

STANDARDS

Some people in England are beginning to realize that while we have been "saving civilization," first from Germans, and then from Bolsheviks, we have come near losing it ourselves.* This disquieting truth has been borne in on them by various signs and portents, not least by the utter collapse of taste. At life's feast we are like people with colds in their heads : we have lost all power of discrimination. As ever, "Dido, Queen of Carthage," and better things than that, are caviare to the general : what is new, and worse, to our most delicate epicures bloater paste is now caviare.

At a London dinner-party even a peeress, even an American lady who has married a peer, dare not commit herself to an adverse literary judgement—except in the case of notoriously disaffected writers—for the very good reason that she does not know where to go for a literary judgement that shall be above reproach. We have as little confidence in our critics as in our ministers. Indeed, since all our officers, and most of our privates, took to publishing pages of verse or, at any rate, of prose that looks odd enough to be verse, the habit of criticism has been voted unpatriotic. To grudge a man in the trenches a column of praise loud enough to drown for a moment the noise of battle would have seemed ungrateful and, what is worse,

* Written in March 1919.

fastidious. Our critics were neither; they did their bit : and no one was surprised to hear the stuff with which schoolboys line their lockers described as " one of the truest, deepest, and most moving notes that have been struck since the days of Elizabeth."

This sort of thing was encouraging at the time, and kept our lads in good heart ; but. in the long run, it has proved demoralizing to our critics as well as to their clients. For, now that the war is over, those who so loyally proclaimed that any bugle-boy was a better musician than any fiddler find themselves incapable of distinguishing, not only between fiddlers, but even between buglers. Perhaps it was natural that when, during the war, T. S. Eliot, about the best of our young poets—if ours I may call him—published *Prufrock*, no English paper, so far as I know, should have given him more than a few words of perfunctory encouragement : natural that when Virginia Woolf, the best of our younger novelists, and Middleton Murry published works of curious imagination and surprising subtlety, critics, worn in the service of Mr. Bennett of the Propaganda Office and our Mr. Wells, should not have noticed that here were a couple of artists : but is it not as strange as sad that our patriot geese, time out of mind a nation's oracles, should still be unable to tell us whether Lieutenant Brooke, Captain Nicholls, Major

Grenfell, or Lieut.-Colonel Maurice Baring is the greatest poet of this age ?

And in painting and music things are no better. Even our old prejudices are gone. All is welcome now, except real art ; and even that gets splashed in the wild outpour of adulation. To admire everything is, perhaps, a more amiable kind of silliness than to admire no-thing : it is silliness all the same. Also, it has brought taste to such a pass that, except the Russian ballet, there was not last winter* in London one entertainment at which a person of reasonable intelligence could bear to spend an hour. As for the ballet, it was a music-hall turn, lasting fifteen minutes, which the public seemed to like rather better than the perform-ing dogs and distinctly less than the ventrilo-quist. The public accepted it because it ac-cepts whatever is provided. Nevertheless, the subtler of our music-hall comedians have obviously been ordered to coarsen their methods or clear out, and the rare jokes that used to re-lieve the merry misery of our revues and plays are now dispensed with as superfluous.

The war is not entirely to blame : the disease was on us long before 1914. War, however, created an atmosphere in which it was bound to prevail. Active service conditions are notori-ously unfavourable to the critical spirit. The army canteen need not tempt its customers :

* The winter 1918-19.

neither need the ordinary shop under a rationing system: and, it must be confessed, the habit of catering for colonial soldiers has not tended to make our public entertainments more subtle or amusing. But the disease of which taste is sick unto death has been on us these fifty years. It is the emporium malady. We are slaves of the trade-mark. Our tastes are imposed on us by our tradesmen, under which respectable title I include newspaper owners, booksellers' touts, book-stall keepers, music-hall kings, opera syndicates, picture-dealers, and honest bagmen.

As for the tradesman, he is no longer an expert any more than the critic or the impressario is. No longer a merchant, no longer a shopkeeper even, he is to-day a universal provider. Fifty years ago the nice housewife still prided herself on knowing the right place for everything. There was a little man in a back street who imported just the coffee she wanted, another who blended tea to perfection, a third who could smoke a ham as a ham should be smoked. All have vanished now; and the housewife betakes herself to the stores. We no longer insist on getting what we like, we like what we get. The March Hare's paradox has ceased to be paradoxical. For five years Europe has been doing what it was told to do; for five years our experts have subjected their critical sense to a sense of patriotism and a desire to keep in with the majority; at last the producers themselves have lost their sense of values and can no longer test the quality of their own productions. There are no standards.

Let no one imagine that standards are, like police regulations, things that can be imposed by authority. Standards exist in the mind, where they grow out of that personal sense of values which is one of the twin pillars on which civilization rests. All that authority can do is to stimulate and sharpen that sense by subtle education and absolute sincerity. The critic can put good things in another man's way and present them in a sympathetic light ; also, he can resolutely refuse ever to pretend that he likes what he does not like. Standards are imposed from above in the sense that people who have the ability and leisure to cultivate their sense of values will, if they take advantage of their opportunities, inevitably influence those less favourably placed. In the fine arts, certainly, taste is bound to be very much directed by people blest with peculiar gifts and armed with special equipment. But, besides taste in the fine arts, there is such a thing as taste in life ; a power of discerning and choosing for one's self in life's minor matters ; and on this taste in life, this sense of the smaller values, is apt to flourish that subtler and more precious æsthetic sense. Without this taste no civilization can exist ; for want of it European civilization is seemingly about to perish.

STANDARDS

Take the thing at its lowest. A rich, good-humoured fellow, replete with a fabulously expensive but distressingly ill-chosen dinner in a magnificently ill-furnished and over-lit restaurant, excited by Saumur (recommended as " Perrier Jouet, 1911 ") and a great deal of poor conversation drowned, for the most part, by even noisier music, may be heard to say, as he permits the slovenly waiter to choose him the most expensive cigar—" That will do, sonny, the best's good enough for me." The best is not good enough for anyone who has standards; but the modern Englishman seems to have none. To go to the most expensive shop and buy the dearest thing there is his notion of getting the best. You may dine at any of the half-dozen " smartest " restaurants in London, pay a couple of pounds for your meal, and be sure that a French commercial traveller, bred to the old standards of the provincial ordinary, would have sent for the cook and given him a scolding. It is not to be supposed that the most expensive English restaurants fail to engage the most expensive French chefs ; they are engaged, but they soon fall below the mark because there is no one to keep them up to it. The clients have no standards. Go to the opera and look at the rich ladies' frocks : they might have come out of an antimacassar factory. They express no sense of what is personally becoming nor a

sense of insolent luxury even : they bear witness to an utter lack of standards, and they cost
a great deal of money. The best is good
enough for these fine ladies, and their best is
the dressmaker's most expensive.

This is no mere question of fashions and conventions. If standards go, civilization goes.
To hear people talk you might suppose there
had never been such things as dark ages. Not
only have there been dark ages, there has been
an unmeasured tract of pre-historic savagery,
and sharp eyes—notably those of Louis Weber
—are beginning to detect certain similarities
between this age and that. The peculiarity of
the historic age, man's brilliant age, the age
of civilization, is the conservatism of its technique and its spiritual restlessness. In the pre-
historic age man's best energies were apparently devoted to perfecting the means to
material existence. Improving the instrument
was the grand preoccupation. From the old
stone age to the new, from that to bronze,
and from bronze to iron is the story of pre-
historic development. Then follow some forty
centuries during which man rests content with
his instrument. Between the Minoan age
and the Industrial Revolution his technical discoveries are insignificant by comparison with
his spiritual adventures. Content with the
plough, the wagon, and the loom, man turns
the sharp edge of his mind to things of the

mind, considers himself in all his relations, thinks, feels, states, expresses, concerns himself with spiritual, rather than material, problems. With the Industrial Revolution begins the third act. Again human intelligence and ingenuity concentrate on the prehistoric problem —the perfecting of the instrument. For a hundred years Europe marches merrily back towards barbarism. Then, at the very moment when she is becoming alarmed and self-critical, at the very moment when she is wondering how she is to reconcile her new material ambitions with the renascent claims of the spirit, comes a war that relegates to the dust-bin or the gaol all that is not of immediate practical utility. The smoke of battle drifts slowly away and reveals a situation almost hopeless. We have lost our standards, our taste in life : we have lost the very thing by which we recognized that there were such things as spiritual values.

In one of his early essays Renan points out that the proper apology for the old French aristocracy is that it performed the proper function of a leisured class. It maintained standards. Unlike the English, it concerned itself neither with politics nor with money-making, nor yet with local affairs : it stood apart, " formant dans la nation une classe qui n'avait d'autre souci que les choses liberales." Renan recognized that a leisured class is the source of civilization ; whether he also recognized that there is no earthly reason why a leisured class should be the ruling class is not clear. In Europe we have now no leisured class; we have only a number of rich men, mere wealth-producers, who perform for high wages the useful functions that miners and milkmaids perform for low ones. Our leisured class, moribund before the war, died peacefully in its sleep the year before last. There is no class on this side the Atlantic to insist on quality now. But if, as I am told, we all owe money to America, has not America acquired, along with her financial supremacy, certain moral obligations? Has she not become the leisured class of the world, and, as such, responsible to civilization for the maintenance of those standards without which civilization falls? If so, it is for America to insist in the fine arts on some measure of talent and intelligence, in society on decent manners, in life on a critical attitude: it is for her to reaffirm those standards of excellence below which neither art nor thought nor manners nor merchandize shall be suffered to fall: for her to teach us once again to be fastidious, to embolden us to say to a poet, a painter, a politician, a newspaper proprietor, or even to a *maître d'hôtel*—"This is not good enough." America possesses the means; she can crack the only whip that carries much conviction nowadays. Whether she has the will to use it is quite another matter.

CRITICISM

(1) *Criticism*

Critics do not exist for artists any more than palæontologists exist for fossils. If both critics and artists could recognize this, how much poorer the world would be in malice and rancour ! To help the artist is no part of a critic's business : artists who cannot help themselves must borrow from other artists. The critic's business is to help the public. With the artist he is not directly concerned : he is concerned only with his finished products. So it is ridiculous for the artist to complain that criticism is unhelpful, and absurd for the critic to read the artist lectures with a view to improving his art. If the critic reads lectures it must be with a view to helping the public to appreciate, not the artist to create. To put the public in the way of æsthetic pleasure, that is the end for which critics exist, and to that end all means are good.

Connoisseurs in pleasure—of whom I count myself one—know that nothing is more intensely delightful than the æsthetic thrill. Now, though many are capable of tasting this pleasure, few can get it for themselves : for only those who have been born with a peculiar sensibility, and have known how to cherish it, enjoy art naturally, simply, and at first hand as most of us enjoy eating, drinking, and kissing. But, fortunately, it is possible for the peculiarly sensitive, or for some of them, by infecting others with their enthusiasm, to throw these into a state of mind in which they, too, can experience the thrill of æsthetic comprehension. And the essence of good criticism is this: that, instead of merely imparting to others the opinions of the critic, it puts them in a state to appreciate the work of art itself. A man blest with peculiar sensibility, who happens also to possess this infecting power, need feel no more shame in becoming a critic than Socrates would have felt in becoming a don. The vocations are much alike. The good critic puts his pupil in the way of enjoying art, the good don or schoolmaster teaches his how to make the most of life ; while bad critics and pedagogues stuff their victims with those most useless of all useless things, facts and opinions.

Primarily, a critic is a sign-post. He points to a work of art and says—" Stop ! Look ! " To do that he must have the sensibility that distinguishes works of art from rubbish, and, amongst works of art, the excellent from the mediocre. Further, the critic has got to convince, he has got to persuade the spectator that there is something before him that is really worth looking at. His own reaction, therefore, must be genuine and intense. Also, he must be able to stimulate an appreciative state of mind ; he must, that is to say, have the art of criticism. He should be able, at a pinch, to disentangle and appraise the qualities which go to make up a masterpiece, so that he may lead a reluctant convert by partial pleasures to a sense of the whole. And, because nothing stands more obstructively between the public and the grand æsthetic ecstasies than the habit of feeling a false emotion for a pseudo-work-of-art, he must be as remorseless in exposing shams as a good schoolmaster would be in exposing charlatans and short-cuts to knowledge.

Since, in all times and places, the essence of art—the externalizing in form of something that lies at the very depths of personality—has been the same, it may seem strange, at first sight, that critical methods should have varied. One moment's reflection will suffice to remind us that there are often ten thousand paths to the same goal ; and a second's may suggest that the variety in critical methods is, at any rate, not more surprising than the variety in the methods of artists. Always have artists been striving to convert the thrill of inspiration into significant form ; never have they stuck long to any one converting-machine. Throughout the ages there has been a continual chopping and changing of " the artistic problem." Canons in criticism are as unessential as subjects in painting. There are ends to which a variety of means are equally good : the artist's end is to create significant form ; that of the critic to bring his spectator before a work of art in an alert and sympathetic frame of mind. If we can realize that Giotto, with his legends, and Picasso, with his cubes, are after the same thing, surely we can understand that when Vasari talks of "Truth to Nature" or "nobility of sentiment," and Mr. Roger Fry of " planes " and " relations," both are about the same business.

Only a fool could suppose that the ancients were less sensitive to art than we are. Since they were capable of producing great art it seems silly to pretend that they were incapable of appreciating it. We need not be dismayed by the stories of Apelles and Polygnotus with their plums and sparrows. These are merely the instruments of criticism : by such crude means did ancient critics excite the public and try to express their own subtle feelings. If anyone seriously believes that the Athenians admired the great figures on the Parthenon for their fidelity to Nature I would invite him to take into consideration the fact that they are not faithful at all. More probably a sensitive Athenian admired them for much the same reasons as we admire them. He felt much what we feel : only, he expressed his admiration and thus provoked the admiration of others, by calling these grand, distorted, or " idealized " figures " lifelike." Reading the incomparable Vasari, one is not more struck by his sensibility and enthusiasm than by the improbability of his having liked the pictures he did like for the childish reasons he is apt to allege. Could anyone be moved by the verisimilitude of Uccello ? I forget whether that is what Vasari commends : what I am sure of is that he was moved by the same beauties that move us.

The fact is, it matters hardly at all what words the critic employs provided they have the power of infecting his audience with his genuine enthusiasm for an authentic work of art. No one can state in words just what he feels about a work of art—especially about a work of visual art. He may exclaim ; indeed, if he be a critic he should exclaim, for that is how he arrests the public. He may go on to seek some rough equivalent in words for his excited feelings. But whatever he may say will amount to little more than steam let off. He cannot describe his feelings ; he can only make it clear that he has them. That is why analytical criticism of painting and music is always beside the mark : neither, I think, is analytical criticism of literary art much more profitable. With literature that is not pure art the case is different, facts and ideas being, of course, the analyst's natural prey. But before a work of art the critic can do little more than jump for joy. And that is all he need do if, like Cherubino, he is " good at jumping." The warmth and truth of Vasari's sentiment

comes straight through all his nonsense.
Because he really felt he can still arrest.

Take an artist who has always been popular,
and see what the ages have had to say about
him. For more than two hundred and fifty
years Poussin has been admired by most of
those who have been born sensitive to the
visual arts. No pretexts could be more diverse
than those alleged by these admirers. Yet it
would be as perverse to suppose that they have
all liked him for totally different reasons as to
maintain that all those who, since the middle
of the seventeenth century, have relished
strawberries have tasted different flavours.
What is more, when I read, say, the fantastic
discourses on the pictures of Poussin delivered
by the Academicians of 1667, I feel certain
that some of these erudite old gentlemen had,
in fact, much the same sort of enthusiasm,
stirred by the monumental qualities of his design and the sober glory of his colours, that I
have myself. Through all the dry dust of
their pedantry the accent of æsthetic sensibility
rings clear.

Poussin's contemporaries praised him chiefly
as a preceptor, an inculcator of historical truths,
more especially the truths of classical and
Hebrew history. That is why Philippe de
Champaigne deplores the fact that in his
Rebecca " Poussin n'ait pas traité le sujet de son
tableau avec toute la fidélité de l'histoire, parce

qu'il a retranché la représentation des chameaux,
dont l'Ecriture fait mention." But Le Brun,
approaching the question from a different angle,
comes heavily down on his scrupulous colleague
with the rejoinder that " M. Poussin a rejeté
les objets bizarres qui pouvaient débaucher
l'œil du spectateur et l'amuser à des minuties."
The philosophic eighteenth century remarked
with approval that Poussin was the exponent
of a wholesome doctrine calculated to advance
the happiness of mankind. But to the fervid
pages of Diderot, wherein that tender enthu-
siast extols Poussin to the skies, asserting that
one finds in his work " le charme de la nature
avec les incidents ou les plus doux ou les plus
terribles de la vie," our modern sensibility
makes no response. And we are right. The
whole panegyric rings hollow. For to visual
art Diderot had no reaction, as every line he
wrote on the subject shows.

That devout critic who, in the reign of the
respectable Louis-Philippe, discovered that
" Nicolas Poussin était doué d'une foi profonde :
la piété fut son seul refuge," is in the same boat.
And for companion they have Mr. Ruskin,
who, being, like them, incapable of a genuine
æsthetic emotion, is likewise incapable of infecting a truly sensitive reader. So far as I
remember, Ruskin's quarrel with Poussin is
that to his picture of the *Flood* he has given a
prevailing air of sobriety and gloom, whereas

it is notorious that an abundance of rain causes all green things to flourish and the rocks to shine like agate. But when Ingres attributes the excellence of Poussin to the fact that he was a faithful disciple of the ancients we feel that he is talking about the thing that matters, and that he is talking sense. And we feel the same—what instance could more prettily illustrate my theory ?—when Delacroix passionately asserts that Poussin was an arch-revolutionary.*

The divergence between the pretexts alleged by our ancestors for their enthusiasm and the reasons given by us, moderns, is easily explained by our intense self-consciousness. We are deeply interested in our own states of mind : we are all psychologists now. From psychology springs the modern interest in æsthetics ; those who care for art and the processes of their own minds finding themselves æstheticians willy-nilly. Now, art-criticism and æsthetics are two things, though at the present moment the former is profoundly influenced by the latter. By works of art we are thrown into an extraordinary state of mind, and, unlike our forefathers, we want to give some exacter account of that state than that it is pleasant, and of the objects that provoke it some more accurate and precise description than that they are lifelike,

* For this little history of Poussin criticism I am indebted to M. Paul Desjardins : *Poussin* (Paris, Librairie Renouard).

or poetical, or beautiful even. We expect our critics to find some plausible cause for so considerable an effect. We ask too much. It is for the æsthetician to analyze a state of mind and account for it : the critic has only to bring into sympathetic contact the object that will provoke the emotion and the mind that can experience it. Therefore, all that is required of him is that he should have sensibility, conviction, and the art of making his conviction felt. Fine sensibility he must have. He must be able to spot good works of art. No amount of eloquence in the critic can give form significance. To create that is the artist's business. It is for the critic to put the public in the way of enjoying it.

2. *Second Thoughts*

It is becoming fashionable to take criticism seriously, or, more exactly, serious critics are trying to make it so. How far they have succeeded may be measured by the fact that we are no longer ashamed to reprint our reviews : how far they are justified is another question. It is one the answer to which must depend a good deal on our answer to that old and irritating query—is beauty absolute ? For, if the function of a critic be merely to perform the office of a sign-post, pointing out what he personally likes and stimulating for that as much enthusiasm as possible, his task is clearly something less priestlike than it would be if, beauty being absolute, it were his to win for absolute beauty adequate appreciation.

I do not disbelieve in absolute beauty any more than I disbelieve in absolute truth. On the contrary, I gladly suppose that the proposition—this object must be either beautiful or not beautiful—is absolutely true. Only, can we recognize it? Certainly, at moments we believe that we can. We believe it when we are taken unawares and bowled over by the purely æsthetic qualities of a work of art. The purely æsthetic qualities, I say, because we can be thrown into that extraordinarily lucid and unself-conscious transport wherein we are aware only of a work of art and our re-action to it by æsthetic qualities alone. Every now and then the beauty, the bald miracle, the "significant form"—if I may venture the phrase—of a picture, a poem, or a piece of music—of something, perhaps, with which we had long believed ourselves familiar—springs from an unexpected quarter and lays us flat. We were not on the look-out for that sort of thing, and we abandon ourselves without one meretricious gesture of welcome. What we feel has nothing to do with a pre-existent mood; we are transported into a world washed clean of all past experience æsthetic or senti-mental. When we have picked ourselves up we begin to suppose that such a state of mind must have been caused by something of which the significance was inherent and the value absolute. "This," we say, "is absolute beauty." Perhaps it is. Only, let us hesitate to give that rather alarming style to anything that has moved us less rapturously or less spontaneously.

For, ninety-nine out of a hundred of our æsthetic experiences have been carefully prepared. Art rarely catches us : we go half way to meet it, we hunt it down even with a pack of critics. In our chastest moments we enter a concert-hall or gallery with the deliberate intention of being moved : in our most abandoned we pick up Browning or Alfred de Musset and allow our egotism to bask in their oblique flattery. Now, when we come to art with a mood of which we expect it to make something brilliant or touching there can be no question of being possessed by absolute beauty. The emotion that we obtain is thrilling enough, and exquisite may be ; but it is self-conscious and reminiscent : it is conditioned. It is conditioned by our mood : what is more—critics please take note—this precedent mood not only colours and conditions our experience, but draws us inevitably towards those works of art in which it scents sympathy and approval. To a reflective moralist Wordsworth will always mean more than a yellow primrose meant to Peter Bell. In our

moments of bitter disillusionment it is such a
comfort to jest with Pope and His Lordship
that we lose all patience with the advanced
politician who prefers Blake. And, behold, we
are in a world of personal predilections, a
thousand miles from absolute values.

Discussion of this question is complicated by
the fact that a belief in the absolute nature of
beauty is generally considered meritorious. It
can be hitched onto, and even made to support,
a disbelief in the theory that the universe is a
whimsical and unpremeditated adventure which
rolls merrily down the road to ruin without
knowing in the least where it is going or caring
to go anywhere in particular. This theory is
unpopular. Wherefore, absolute beauty is too
often fitted into a whole system of absolutes,
or rather into The Absolute ; and, of course,
it would be intolerable to suppose that we could
ever fail to recognize—should I say Him ?
Unluckily, history and personal experience—
those two black beasts of *a priori* idealists—
here await us. If beauty be absolute, the past
was sometimes insensitive, or we are : for the
past failed to recognize the beauty of much
that seems to us supremely beautiful, and sincerely admired much that to us seems trash.
And we, ourselves, did we never despise what
to-day we adore ? Murillo and Salvator Rosa
and forgers of works by both enjoyed for years
the passionate admiration of the *cognoscenti*.

In Dr. Johnson's time " no composition in our language had been oftener perused than Pomfret's *Choice*." If ever there was a man who should have been incapable of going wrong about poetry that man was Thomas Gray. How shall we explain his enthusiasm for Macpherson's fraud ? And if there be another of whom the bowling over might be taken as conclusive evidence in the court of literary appeal that other is surely Coleridge. Hark to him : " My earliest acquaintances will not have forgotten the undisciplined eagerness and impetuous zeal with which I laboured to make proselytes, not only of my companions, but of all with whom I conversed, of whatever rank, and in whatever place. . . . And with almost equal delight did I receive the three or four following publications of the same author." That author was the Reverend Mr. Bowles.

I was saying that any work of art that has given the authentic thrill to a man of real sensibility must have an absolute and inherent value : and, of course, we all are really sensitive. Only, it is sometimes difficult to be sure that our thrill was the real *coup de foudre* and not the mere gratification of a personal appetite. Let us admit so much : let us admit that we do sometimes mistake what happens to suit us for what is absolutely and universally good ; which once admitted, it will be easy to concede further that no one can hope to recognize all manifestations of beauty. History is adamant against any other conclusion. No one can quite escape his age, his civilization, and his peculiar disposition ; from which it seems to follow that not even the unanimous censure of generations can utterly discredit anything. The admission comes in the nick of time : history was on the point of calling attention to the attitude of the seventeenth and eighteenth centuries to Gothic, Romanesque, and Byzantine art.

The fact is, most of our enthusiasms and antipathies are the bastard offspring of a pure æsthetic sense and a permanent disposition or a transitory mood. The best of us start with a temperament and a point of view, the worst with a cut-and-dried theory of life ; and for the artist who can flatter and intensify these we have a singular kindness, while to him who appears indifferent or hostile it is hard to be even just. What is more, those who are most sensitive to art are apt to be most sensitive to these wretched, irrelevant implications. They pry so deeply into a work that they cannot help sometimes spying on the author behind it. And remember, though rightly we set high and apart that supreme rapture in which we are carried to a world of impersonal and disinterested admiration, our æsthetic experience would be small indeed were it confined to this. More often than not it must be of works that have moved him partly by matching a mood that the best of critics writes.   More often than not he is disentangling and exhibiting qualities of which all he can truly say is that they have proved comfortable or exhilarating to a particular person at a particular moment.   He is dealing with matters of taste ; and about tastes, you know, *non est disputandum*.

I shall not pretend that when I call the poetry of Milton good I suppose my judgement to have no more validity than what may be claimed for that of the urchin who says the same of peppermints : but I do think a critic should cultivate a sense of humour.   If he be very sure that his enthusiasm is the only appropriate response of a perfectly disinterested sensibility to absolute beauty, let him be as dogmatic as is compatible with good breeding : failing that, I counsel as great a measure of modesty as may be compatible with the literary character.   Let him remember that, as a rule, he is not demanding homage for what he knows to be absolutely good, but pointing to what he likes and trying to explain why he likes it.   That, to my mind, is the chief function of a critic.   After all, an unerring eye for masterpieces is perhaps of more use to a dealer than to him.   Mistakes do not matter much : if we are to call mistakes what are very likely no more than the records of a perverse or obscure mood.   Was it a mistake in 1890 to rave about Wagner ?   Is it a mistake to find him intolerable now ?   Frankly, I suspect the

man or woman of the nineties who was un-
moved by Wagner of having wanted sensibility,
and him or her who to-day revels in that music
of being æsthetically oversexed. Be that as it
may, never to pretend to like what bores or
dislike what pleases him, to be honest in his reactions and exact in their description, is all I now
ask of a critic. It is asking a good deal, I think.
To a lady who protested that she knew what she
liked, Whistler is said to have replied—" So,
madame, do the beasts of the field." Do
they ? Then all I can say is the beasts of the
field are more highly developed than most of
the ladies and gentlemen who write about art
in the papers.

3. *Last Thoughts*

Already I am in a scrape with the critics. I
am in a scrape for having said, a couple of
years ago, that a critic was nothing but a sign-
post, and for having added, somewhat later,
that he was a fallible sign-post at that. So
now, contributing to a supplement * which,
being written by critics, is sure to be read by
them, I naturally take the opportunity of explaining that what I said, if rightly understood,
was perfectly civil and obliging.

Perhaps I shall stand a better chance of
pardon when it is perceived that I, too, am

* Contributed to the Critical Supplement of *The New
Republic*.

fallible, and, what is more, that I am quite aware of the fact. The reader can see for himself that, from first thoughts to last— in three years, that is—not only have my opinions on the art of criticism been modified, but my critical opinions have themselves become less confident. So, to recall what I did say : I said that critics exist for the public, and that it is no part of their business to help artists with good advice. I argued that a critic no more exists for artists than a palæontologist does for the Dinosaurs on whose fossils he expatiates, and that, though artists happen to create those exciting objects which are the matter of a critic's discourse, that discourse is all for the benefit of the critic's readers. For these, I said, he is to procure æsthetic pleasures : and his existence is made necessary by the curious fact that, though works of art are charged with a power of provoking extraordinarily intense and desirable emotions, the most sensitive people are often incapable of experiencing them until a jog or a drop of stimulant even has been given to their appreciative faculties.

A critic should be a guide and an animator. His it is first to bring his reader into the presence of what he believes to be art, then to cajole or bully him into a receptive frame of mind. He must, therefore, besides conviction, possess a power of persuasion and stimulation ; and if anyone imagines that these are common or contemptible gifts he mistakes. It would, of course, be much nicer to think that the essential part of a critic's work was the discovery and glorification of absolute beauty : only, unluckily, it is far from certain that absolute beauty exists, and most unlikely, if it does, that any human being can distinguish it from what is relative. The wiser course, therefore, is to ask of critics no more than sincerity, and to leave divine certitude to superior beings—magistrates, for instance, and curates, and fathers of large families, and Mr. Bernard Shaw. At any rate, it is imprudent, I am sure, in us critics to maintain so stoutly as we are apt to do, that when we call a work of art " good " we do not mean simply that we like it with passion and conviction but that it is absolutely so, seeing that the most sensitive people of one age have ever extolled some things which the most sensitive of another have cried down, and have cried down what others have extolled. And, indeed, I will bet whatever this essay may be worth that there is not a single contributor to this supplement who would not flatly contradict a vast number of the æsthetic judgements which have been pronounced with equal confidence by the most illustrious of his predecessors. No critic can be sure that what he likes has absolute value ; and it is a mark of mere silliness to suppose that what he dislikes can have no value at all. Neither is there any need of certainty. A critic must have sincerity and conviction— he must be convinced of the genuineness of his own feelings. Never may he pretend to feel more or less or something other than what he does feel ; and what he feels he should be able to indicate, and even, to some extent, account for. Finally, he must have the power of infecting others with his own enthusiasm. Anyone who possesses these qualities and can do these things I call a good critic.

" And what about discrimination ? " says someone. " What about the very meaning of the word ? " Certainly the power of discriminating between artists, that of discriminating between the parts and qualities of a work of art, and the still different power of discriminating between one's own reactions, are important instruments of criticism ; but they are not the only ones, nor, I believe, are they indispensable. At any rate, if the proper end of criticism be the fullest appreciation of art, if the function of a critic be the stimulation of the reader's power of comprehending and enjoying, all means to that end must be good. The rest of this essay will be devoted to a consideration of the means most commonly employed.

Discriminating critics, as opposed to those other two great classes—the Impressionistic and the Biographical—are peculiar in this amongst other things : they alone extract light from refuse and deal profitably with bad art. I am not going back on my axiom—the proper end of criticism is appreciation : but I must observe that one means of stimulating a taste for what is most excellent is an elaborate dissection of what is not. I remember walking with an eminent contributor to *The New Republic* and a lady who admired so intemperately the writings of Rupert Brooke that our companion was at last provoked into analyzing them with magisterial severity. He concluded by observing that a comparison of the more airy and fantastic productions of this gallant young author with the poems of Andrew Marvell would have the instant effect of putting the former in their place. The lady took the hint ; and has since confessed that never before had she so clearly seen or thoroughly enjoyed the peculiar beauties, the sweetness, the artful simplicity and sly whimsicality of the most enchanting of English poets. The discriminating critic is not afraid of classifying artists and putting them in their places. Analysis is one of his most precious instruments. He will pose the question—" Why is Milton a great poet ? "—and will proceed to disengage certain definite qualities the existence of which can be proved by demonstration and handled objectively with almost scientific precision. This sort of criticism was brought to perfection in the eighteenth century; and certainly it did sometimes lead critics quite out of sight and reach of the living spirit of poetry. It was responsible for masses of amazing obtuseness (especially in criticism of the visual arts); it was the frequent cause of downright silliness; it made it possible for Dr. Johnson, commenting on the line *Time and the hour runs through the roughest day*, to " suppose every reader is disgusted at the tautology "; but it performed the immense service of stimulating enthusiasm for clear thought and exact expression. These discriminating and objective critics will always be particularly useful to those whose intellects dominate their emotions, and who need some sort of intellectual jolt to set their æsthetic sensibilities going. Happily, the race shows no signs of becoming extinct, and Sir Walter Raleigh and M. Lanson are the by no means unworthy successors of Dr. Johnson and Saint-Evremond.

It is inexact to say that the nineteenth century invented impressionist criticism, the nineteenth century invented nothing except the electric light and Queen Victoria. But it was in the later years of that century that Impressionism became self-conscious and pompous enough to array itself in a theory. The method everyone knows : the critic clears his mind of general ideas, of canons of art, and, so far as possible, of all knowledge of good and evil; he gets what emotions he can from the work before him, and then confides them to the public.* He does not attempt to criticize in the literal sense of the word ; he merely tells us what a book, a picture, or a piece of music makes him feel. This method can be intensely exciting ; what is more, it has made vast additions to our æsthetic experience. It is the instrument that goes deepest : sometimes it goes too deep, passes clean through the object of contemplation, and brings up from the writer's own consciousness something for which in the work itself no answerable provocation is to be found. This leads, of course, to disappointment and vexation, or else to common dishonesty, and can add nothing to the reader's appreciation. On the other hand, there are in some works of art subtleties and adumbrations hardly to be disentangled by any other means. In much of the best modern poetry—since Dante and Chaucer, I mean—there are beauties

---

* Happily, I have never laid great claims to that prevalent modern virtue, originality; otherwise, I might have been somewhat dashed by coming across the following passage, only the other day, in the miscellaneous writings of Gibbon (*de mes lectures Oct.* 3, 1762): " Till now (says he) I was acquainted only with two ways of criticising a beautiful passage : the one, to shew, by an exact anatomy of it, the distinct beauties of it, and whence they sprung; the other, an idle exclamation, or a general encomium which leaves nothing behind it. Longinus has shewn me that there is a third. He tells me his own feelings upon reading it; and tells them with such energy that he communicates them."

which would rarely have been apprehended had not someone, throwing the whole apparatus of objective criticism aside, vividly described, not the beauties themselves, but what they made him feel. And I will go so far as to admit that in a work of art there may be qualities, significant and precious, but so recondite and elusive that we shall hardly grasp them unless some adventurer, guided by his own experience, can trace their progress and show us their roots in the mind from which they sprang.

Impressionistic criticism of literature is not much approved nowadays, though Mr. Arthur Symonds and one or two of his contemporaries still preserve it from the last outrages of a new and possibly less subtle generation, while M. Proust, by using it to fine effect in his extraordinary masterpiece, may even bring it again into fashion. But it has got a bad name by keeping low company ; for it has come to be associated with those journalistic reviewers who describe, not the feelings and ideas provoked in them by reading a book, but what they thought and felt and did at or about the time they were supposed to be reading it. These are the chatterboxes who will tell you how they got up, cut themselves shaving, ate sausages, spilt the tea, and nearly missed the train in which they began to read the latest work of Benedetto Croce, which, unluckily, having got into conversation with a pretty typist or a humorous bagman, they quite forgot, left in the carriage, and so can tell you no more about. But this is not Impressionism, it is mere vulgarity.

If in literary criticism the impressionist method is falling into disfavour, in the criticism of music and painting it holds the field. Nor is this surprising : to write objectively about a symphony or a picture, to seize its peculiar intrinsic qualities and describe them exactly in words, is a feat beyond the power of most. Wherefore, as a rule, the unfortunate critic must either discourse on history, archæology, and psychology, or chatter about his own feelings. With the exception of Mr. Roger Fry there is not in England one critic capable of saying so much, to the purpose, about the intrinsic qualities of a work of visual art as half a dozen or more—Sir Walter Raleigh, Mr. Murry, Mr. Squire, Mr. Clutton Brock, Sir Arthur Quiller-Couch, and Mr. McCarthy to begin with—can be trusted to say easily, and, if necessary, weekly, about the intrinsic qualities of a book. To be sure, Mr. Fry is a great exception : with my own ears have I heard him take two or three normally intelligent people through a gallery and by severely objective means provoke in them a perfect frenzy of enthusiasm for masterpieces of utterly different schools and ages. Doubtless that is what art-criticism should be ; but perhaps it is wrong to despise utterly those who achieve something less.

Just at present it is the thing to laugh at biographical and historical critics, a class of which Sainte-Beuve is the obvious representative, and to which belong such writers as Taine and Francesco de Sanctis and all who try to explain works of art by describing their social and political circumstances. " At any rate," it is said, " these are not *critics*." I shall not quarrel over words ; but I am persuaded that, when they care genuinely for books and have a gift of exposition, these perform the same function as their more æsthetically-minded brethren. I am sure that a *causerie* by Sainte-Beuve often sends a reader, with a zest he had never found unaided, to a book he had never opened unadvised. There are plenty of men and women, equipped to relish the finest and subtlest things in literature, who can hardly come at a book save through its author, or at an author save through the story of his life and a picture of his surroundings ; wherefore, few things do more to promote and disseminate a taste for art and letters and, I will add, for all things of the spirit, than biographical and historical criticism and the discussion of tendencies and ideas.

And this brings me to my conclusion. Though the immediate object of criticism is to put readers in the way of appreciating fully a work or works in the merit of which the critic believes, its ultimate value lies further afield in more general effects. Good criticism not only puts people in the way of appreciating particular works ; it makes them feel, it makes them remember, what intense and surprising pleasures are peculiar to the life of the spirit. For these it creates an appetite, and keeps that appetite sharp : and I would seriously advise anyone who complains that his taste for reading has deserted him to take a dip into the great critics and biographers and see whether they will not send him back to his books. For, though books, pictures, and music stand charged with a mysterious power of delighting and exciting and enhancing the value of life ; though they are the keys that unlock the door to the world of the spirit—the world that is best worth living in, busy men and women soon forget. It is for critics to be ever jogging their memories. Theirs it is to point the road and hold open the unlocked doors. In that way they become officers in the kingdom of the mind, or, to use a humbler and preferable term, essential instruments of culture.

OTHON FRIESZ

Friesz is a painter who has " come on " visibly since the war. He has drawn right away from " the field " to join those leaders—Matisse, Picasso, Derain, Bonnard, shall we say, with one or two more in close attendance—a cursory glance at whom, as they flash by, provokes this not unprofitable exclamation : " How different they are ! " Apparently, amongst the chiefs, that famous movement no longer counts for much. Look at them ; to an eye at all practised these artists are as unlike each other as are hounds to the eye of a huntsman. Certainly, they all owe something to Cézanne : but what other important characteristic have they in common which they do not share with the best of the last hundred years ? It was ever thus : the best, who are all alike in some ways, in others are, from the first, the most sharply differentiated simply because they are the most personal. Also, as they mature they become more and more peculiar because they tend to rely less and less on anything but themselves and the grand tradition. Each creates and inhabits a world of his own, which, by the way, he is apt to mistake for the world of everyone who is not maliciously prejudiced against him. And Friesz, whose character and intelligence are utterly unlike those of his compeers, is now, naturally enough, producing work which has little in common with that even of Matisse—

Matisse, to whom, not fifteen years ago, I saw a picture of his attributed by a competent amateur who was the friend of both.

Friesz has an air of being more professional than any other artist of this first rank—for Marchand, I think, is not quite of it. Indeed, for a moment, Friesz may appear alarmingly professional. Certainly, he leaves nothing to chance : all is planned, and planned not in haste and agitation, fingers itching to be at it, but with the deliberation, the critical thoroughness, of an engineer or an architect. There is so much of the painstaking craftsman in his method that for a moment you may overlook the sensitive artist who conceives and executes. But, in fact, the effective alliance of practical intelligence with fine sensibility is the secret of his strength, as I realized one day, when I had the privilege of studying a large decoration (a sketch for a fragment of which is to be seen in this exhibition)* which Friesz had just carried out. Since then I have not doubted that he was the man who might give this age that of which the age talks much and gets little —monumental decoration.

Large decorative schemes—when they are not, what most are, mere wastes of tumid pomposity—are apt to fail for one of two reasons : either they are too much like pictures or too little like works of art. Because very

* At the Independent Gallery, 1921.

few artists are capable by taking thought of
adapting their means to an unfamiliar end, it
will happen that a sensitive and gifted painter
sets about a decoration as though he were
beginning an easel picture. He has his sense
of the importance of richness, of filling a picture to the brim ; he has a technique adequate
to his conception ; but he has neither the
practical readiness nor the intellectual robust-
ness which would enable him to adjust these
to a new problem. He endeavours, therefore,
to key every part of his scheme up to the highest
pitch of intensity that line and colour can bear.
He is attempting the impossible ; his conception is inappropriate ; and, in any case, his
technique is unequal to so vast an undertaking.
He produces something which may be delicious
in detail but is pretty sure to be unsatisfactory
as a whole. He fails to fill his space. His
work has the vice of Sidney's *Arcadia* and the
Religio Medici : it is good to dip into. You
cannot write an epic as though it were a sonnet.

On the other hand, you must not write an
epic as though you were telling a tale in the bar-
parlour, lest you should create another *Earthly
Paradise*, leaving quite untouched the subtler
and more energetic chords in your listener's
appreciative faculty. The craftsman decorator,
though he may know how to fill vast spaces,
will never fill them with lively images. His
plan may be cleverly devised to surmount

difficulties of structure and material ; it will not be inspired. Incapable of keying his instrument too high, he will be satisfied with a slack string and abominable flatness. His forms will be conventional ; his handling impersonal ; ten to one he will give us a row of insipid Gothic figures or something in the pseudo-Veronese taste.

Almost everyone would admit that, considered as pictures, those great decorations in the Doges' Palace were a little empty; no one can deny that as parts of a vast scheme they are superbly adequate. Very much the same might be said of the decorations I have in mind. It is clear that Friesz plotted and reasoned with himself until he had contrived a method of matching means with ends. By constructing it out of forms less charged, more fluent, and more in the nature of arabesques than those he habitually employs he gave to his scheme continuity and easy comprehensibility : but never did he allow those forms to subside into mere coloured spaces, or the lines to become mere flourishes : always every detail was doing something, and so the whole was significant and alive. The scheme which was planned with caution was carried through with passion.

Now, obviously, a painter capable of performing this feat must possess a rare, at this moment possibly unique, gift. Friesz is one who can bring the whole weight of his intellect to bear on his sensibility. That sensibility let no one underrate. Before his vision of the external world, especially before what we are pleased to call Nature, Friesz has a reaction as delicate and enthusiastic as that of an English poet. Only, unlike most English painters, he would never dream of jotting it down and leaving it at that. Such hit-or-miss frivolity is not in his way. He is no amateur. He takes his impressions home and elaborates them ; he brings his intellect to bear on them ; and, as this exhibition shows, without robbing them of their bloom, makes of them something solid and satisfying. To realize what a power this is we may, I hope without indiscretion, glance for an instant at another handsomely endowed French painter. That M. Lhote does not want for sensibility is shown by his sketches and water-colours, that his intellect is sharp enough is proved by his writings ; but the devitalized rectitude of his more ambitious pieces shows how appallingly difficult it is to bring intellect to bear on sensibility without crushing it. The failure of M. Lhote is the measure of M. Friesz's achievement.

If I am right, it is only natural that pictures by Friesz should improve on acquaintance. The studied logic of the composition may for a time absorb the spectator's attention and blind him to more endearing qualities ; but, sooner or later, he will begin to perceive not only that a scrupulously honest vision has been converted into a well-knit design, but that the stitches are lovely. In every part he will be discovering subtle and seductive harmonies and balances of which the delicacy dawns on him as he gazes. The more he looks the more will he get of that curiously gratifying thrill which comes of the recognition of unostentatious rightness.

But, though he offers the sensitive amateur an unusually generous allowance of the amateur's most delicate pleasure, Friesz is, above all, a painters' painter. He has been called a theorist. And, because he is a painter of exceptionally good understanding, who thinks logically about his art and can find words for what he thinks, I suppose the appellation is admissible. But, remember, he never dreams of trying to convert his theories of art into theories of life. His are not of the kind that can be so converted; I said he was a painters', not a journalists', painter. Also, unlike the theories of the mere craftsman, his are based always on the assumption that there is such a thing as art —something that is created by and appeals to peculiar faculties, something rare and personal, something not to be had simply by taking thought and pains, something as utterly unlike honest craftsmanship as it is unlike the cryptic mutterings of boozy mountebanks: subject, however, to this assumption, his theories are severely practical. They have to do solely with the art of painting ; they are born of his own experience ; and he makes visible use of them. That is why I call Friesz a painters' painter. I wonder whether the Italian Primitives, with that disquietingly unself-conscious inspiration of theirs, directed with such amazing confidence along well devised, practical channels, were not a little like him.

The exhibition is fairly representative of Friesz's later work ; and if it cannot be said quite to summarize a stage of his career, at least it is a milestone. Friesz has arrived : that is to say, what he has already achieved suffices to affirm the existence of a distinct, personal talent entitled to its place in the republic of painting. At that point we leave him. But we may be sure that, with his re-markable gift and even more remarkable power of turning it to account, his energy, his patience, and his manifest ambition, he will soon have gone beyond it.

WILCOXISM

To return from Paris, full of enthusiasm for contemporary art, and find oneself forced immediately into an attitude of querulous hostility is surely a melancholy thing. It is my fate; but it is not my fault. Had I found our native quidnuncs in a slightly less exalted humour, had they gushed a little less over their imperial painters at Burlington House, had they made the least effort to preserve a sense of proportion, I, for my part, had held my peace. But, deafened by the chorus of hearty self-applause with which British art has just been regaling itself,* a critic who hopes that his country is not once again going to make itself the laughing-stock of Europe is bound at all risks to say something disagreeable.

In that delightful book *The Worlds and I*, for bringing me acquainted with which I shall ever be grateful to *The Athenæum*, nothing is more delightful than the chapter in which Mrs. Wilcox takes us through the list of the great writers she has known. We are almost as much pleased by the authoress's confident expectation that we shall be thrilled to learn any new fact about Miss Aldrich, who wrote " one of the most exquisite lyrics in the language "; about Rhoda Hero Dunn, " a genius " with " an almost Shakespearean quality in her verse," or about Elsa Barker, whose poem

* February 1920.

The Frozen Grail, " dedicated to Peary and his band, is an epic of august beauty," and whose sonnet *When I am Dead* " ranks with the great sonnets of the world," as she would be surprised to discover that we had never heard of one of them. Mrs. Wilcox believed, in perfect good faith, that the crowd of magazine-makers with whom she associated were, in fact, the great figures of the age. She had no reason for supposing that we should not be as much interested in first-hand personal gossip about Zona Gale and Ridgeley Torrence, Arthur Grissom (first editor of the *Smart Set*), Judge Malone, Theodosia Garrison, and Julie Opp Faversham (" even to talk with whom over the telephone gives me a sense of larger horizons ") as we should have been in similar gossip about Swinburne and Hardy, Henry James and Mallarmé, Laforgue, Anatole France, Tolstoy, Tchehov, or Dostoevsky.

And, as Mrs. Wilcox had no reason for supposing that her friends were not the greatest writers alive, what reason had she for supposing that they were not the greatest that ever lived ? Without the taste, the intelligence, or the knowledge which alone can give some notion of what's what in art, she was obliged to rely on more accessible criteria. The circulation of her own works, for instance, must have compared favourably with that of most poets. To be sure there was Shakespeare and the cele-

brated Hugo—or was it Gambetta? But
what grounds could there be for thinking that
she was not superior to the obscure John Donne
or the obscurer Andrew Marvel, or to Arthur
Rimbaud, of whom no one she had ever heard
of had ever heard? Mrs. Wilcox was not
dishonest in assuming that the most successful
writer in her set was the best in the world;
she was not conceited even; she was merely
ridiculous.

It is disquieting to find the same sort of thing
going on in England, where our painters are
fiercely disputing with each other the crown
of European painting, and our critics appraising the respective claims of Mr. Augustus John
and Mr. John Nash as solemnly as if they were
comparing Cézanne with Renoir. It is more
than disquieting, it is alarming, to detect symp-
toms of the disease—this distressing disease of
Wilcoxism—in *The Athenæum* itself. Yet I
am positive that not long since I read in this
very paper that Mr. Wyndham Lewis was
more than a match for Matisse and Derain;
and, having said so much, the critic not un-
naturally went on to suggest that he was a
match for Lionardo da Vinci. Since then I
have trembled weekly lest the infection should
have spread to our literary parts. Will it be
asserted, one of these Fridays, that the appetizing novels of Mr. Gilbert Cannan are distinctly better than Hardy's Wessex tales, and

comparable rather with the works of Jane Austen ?

To save ourselves from absurdity, and still more to save our painters from inspissating that trickle of fatuity which wells from heads swollen with hot air, critics should set themselves to check this nasty malady. Let them make it clear that to talk of modern English painting as though it were the rival of modern French is silly. In old racing days—how matters stand now I know not—it used to be held that French form was about seven pounds below English : the winner of the Derby, that is to say, could generally give the best French colt about that weight and a beating. In painting, English form is normally a stone below French. At any given moment the best painter in England is unlikely to be better than a first-rate man in the French second class. Whistler was never a match for Renoir, Degas, Seurat, and Manet ; but Whistler, Steer, and Sickert may profitably be compared with Boudin, Jongkind, and Berthe Morisot. And though Duncan Grant holds his own handsomely with Marchand, Vlaminck, Lhote, de Segonzac, Bracque and Modigliani, I am not yet prepared to class him with Matisse, Picasso, Derain, and Bonnard.

Having bravely recognized this disagreeable truth, let us take as much interest in contemporary British painting as we can. I will try to believe that it merits more enthusiasm than I have been able to show, provided it is not made a point of patriotism to excite oneself about the Imperial War Museum's pictures exhibited at Burlington House. As a matter of fact, the most depressing thing about that show was the absence of the very quality for which British art has been most justly admired —I mean sensibility. Mr. Wilson Steer's picture seemed to me the best in the place, just because Mr. Steer has eyes with which, not only to see, but to feel. To see is something ; Mr. Steer also feels for what he sees ; and this emotion is the point of departure for his pictures. That he seems almost completely to have lost such power as he ever had of giving to his vision a coherent and self-supporting form is unfortunate ; still, he does convey to us some modicum of the thrill provoked in him by his vision of Dover Harbour.

Those thoughtful young men, on the other hand, whose works have been causing such a commotion might almost as well have been blind. They seem to have seen nothing ; at any rate, they have not reacted to what they saw in that particular way in which visual artists react. They are not expressing what they feel for something that has moved them as artists, but, rather, what they think about something that has horrified them as men. Their pictures depart, not from a visual sensa-

tion, but from a moral conviction. So, naturally enough, what they produce is mere " arty "
anecdote. This, perhaps, is the secret of their
success—their success, I mean, with the cultivated public. Those terrible young fellows
who were feared to be artists turn out after all
to be innocent Pre-Raphaelites. They leave
Burlington House without a stain upon their
characters.

This is plain speaking ; how else should a
critic, who believes that he has diagnosed the
disease, convince a modern patient of his par-
lous state ? To just hint a fault and hesitate
dislike (not Pope, but I split that infinitive)
is regarded nowadays merely as a sign of a base,
compromising spirit ; or not regarded at all.
Artists, especially in England, cannot away
with qualified praise or blame : and if they insist on all or nothing I can but offer them the
latter. Nevertheless, I must assert, for my
own satisfaction, that in many even of our most
imperial artists, in the brothers Spenser and the
brothers Nash, in Mr. Lewis, Mr. Roberts,
Mr. Bomberg, and Mr. Lamb, I discover
plenty of ability ; only I cannot help fancying
that they may have mistaken the nature of their
gifts. Were they really born to be painters ?
I wonder. But of this I am sure : their friends
merely make them look silly by comparing
them with contemporary French masters, or
even with Leonardo da Vinci.

WILCOXISM

Wilcoxism is a terrible disease because it slowly but surely eats away our sense of imperfection, our desire for improvement, and our power of self-criticism. Modesty and knowledge are the best antidotes ; and a treatment much recommended by the faculty is to take more interest in art and less in one's own prestige. Above all, let us cultivate a sense of proportion. Let us admire, for instance, the admirable, though somewhat negative, qualities in the work of Mr. Lewis—the absence of vulgarity and false sentiment, the sobriety of colour, the painstaking search for design— without forgetting that in the Salon d'Automne or the Salon des Indépendants a picture by him would neither merit nor obtain from the most generous critic more than a passing word of perfunctory encouragement ; for in Paris there are perhaps five hundred men and women— drawn from the four quarters of the earth—all trying to do what Mr. Lewis tries to do, and doing it better.

ART AND POLITICS

Mr. Roger Fry, by means of an instructive tale (*Athenæum*, August 13, 1920), has shown us that in their dealings with art Bolshevik politicians remain true to type. Like the rest of their breed, they have no use for it unless they can exploit it to their own ends. For my part, I was never so simple as to suppose that, if the *de facto* government of Russia professed admiration for Matisse and Picasso, that admiration had anything to do with the artistic gifts of either of these painters, any more than that the respect with which the British Government treats the names of Raphael and Michel Angelo should be taken to imply that any single one of His Majesty's ministers has ever experienced an æsthetic emotion. Consequently, I was not at all surprised to learn that the sure, though unconscious, taste of the statesman had led the rulers of Russia to reject their first loves; that instinctively they had divined that both Matisse and Picasso were too much like genuine artists to be trustworthy; and that they had, therefore, transferred their affections to the thin, and fundamentally academic, work of Larionoff, which should, I fancy, be just the thing for advanced politicians.

Some time ago, however, before Picasso was found out, a young Russian æsthete—so Mr. Fry tells us—was licensed by the competent authority to pronounce that artist's eulogy, on the understanding, of course, that the lecture should somehow serve as a stick wherewith to beat the opposition. Nothing easier : Picasso was pitted against Renoir. Picasso was a great artist, because, abstract and austere, he was the man for the proletariat ; whereas Renoir, who painted pretty pictures for the *bourgeoisie*, was no earthly good. The lecturer, as might have been expected, was out even in his facts : for Renoir—who came from the people, by the way —might, were he less of an artist, by means of the taking and almost anecdotic quality of his earlier work, give some pleasure to a working man ; whereas Picasso—the son of middle-class parents, too—could not possibly win from an honest labourer, left to himself, anything but sarcastic laughter or ferocious abuse. But even if true, the lecturer's facts would have been beside the point. To say that a work is aristocratic or democratic, moral or immoral, is to say something silly and irrelevant, or rather, silly if meant to be relevant to its value as art. In the work of Renoir and of Picasso, in all works of art for that matter, the essential quality, as every sensitive person knows, is the same. Whatever it may be that makes art matter is to be found in every work that does matter. And though, no doubt, "subject" and to some extent "attack" may be conditioned by an artist's opinions and attitude to life, such things are irrelevant to his work's final significance.

Strange as it may seem, the essential quality in a work of art is purely artistic. It has nothing to do with the moral, religious, or political views of its creator. It has to do solely with his æsthetic experience and his power of expressing that. But, as no politician is capable of appreciating, or even becoming aware of, this essential quality, it is perhaps only natural that politicians should look elsewhere for the significance of art.

This painful but certain fact once grasped, it becomes possible to understand several things that have considerably puzzled critics and historians. For instance, it is often remarked, and generally with surprise, that progressive politicians are commonly averse from new movements in art. The attitude of the present Russian Government to the contemporary movement makes neither for nor against this view, for that novelty it took over as a going concern. Let us see how it looks on the next, which will be very likely a return to the tradition of Ingres. The example usually cited by exponents of this theory—that progressive politicians are reactionary in art—is the notorious hostility of Liberals to the romantic movement ; but I believe that were they to study closely the histories of the Impressionist, the Pre-Raphaelite, and the Wagnerian movements they would find in them, too, evidence on the whole favourable to their case. Be that as it may, this theory, which once seemed paradoxical, quite loses its fantastic air when considered in the light of our discovery. Had art anything to do with opinion it would be strange, indeed, if new art were ill-received by those who like their opinions new. But as art has nothing whatever to do with such things there is no more reason why a Radical should like new forms of art than why he should like new brands of tea.

The essential qualities of a work of art are purely artistic ; and since politicians, if not too coarse by nature, soon make themselves so by practice, to apprehend these they must, unless they can leave art alone, seek its significance in what is unessential. Progressive politicians, who have a way of taking ethics under their wing and even conceive themselves the active promoters of good, are apt to seek it in morals. One might have supposed that a message was to be found as easily in new forms of art as in old ; but, unluckily, new forms are to most incomprehensible. And though to a hardened sinner here and there what is incomprehensible may be nothing worse than disconcerting, to him who seeks good in all things, and is constantly on the look-out for uplifting influences, whatever disappoints this longing is positively and terribly evil. Now, a new and genuine work of art is something unmistakably alive and, at the same time, unprovided, as yet, with moral credentials. It is unintelligible without being negligible. It comes from an unfamiliar world and shakes a good man's belief in the obvious. It must be very wicked. And the proper reaction to what is wicked is a blind fury of moral indignation. Well, blind fury is blind. So no one could be much worse placed than the political moralist for seeing whatever there may be to be seen in what is, at once, strange and subtle.

We are in a position now to clear up another difficulty, which has distressed so deeply the best and wisest of men that to get rid of it some have felt justified in tampering with the truth. If art had anything to do with politics, evidently art should have flourished most gloriously in those ages of political freedom which do us all so much credit. The necessity of this inference has been felt strongly enough by Liberal historians to make them accept without demur the doctrine that the age of Pericles was the great age of visual art, and repeat it without mentioning the fact that in that age an aristocracy of some twenty-five thousand citizens was supported by the compulsory labours of some four hundred thousand slaves. The truth is, of course, that art may flourish under any form of government. It flourished in the Athenian aristocracy and under the despotic bureaucracies of China, Persia, and Byzantium. In the eleventh and twelfth centuries it flourished under the feudal system, and in the fifteenth amongst the oligarchies and tyrannies of Italy. On the other hand, neither the Roman Republic nor the Roman Empire gave us anything much worth remembering : and no period in French history has been less fruitful in art and letters than the first republic and empire. There was Ingres, of course ; but the period on the whole was singularly barren, and it may be just worth remarking that at no time, perhaps, has French art been so academic, professorial, timid, and uninspired as in the first glorious years of the great Revolution.

Here there is nothing to surprise us. But what does, at first sight, seem odd is that art should apparently be indifferent, not only to political systems, but to social conditions as well. Barbarism or Civilization : it is all one to art. Old-fashioned historians, who had a pleasant, tidy way of dealing with the past, used to plot out from that wilderness four great periods of civilization : the Athenian (from 480 B.C. to the death of Aristotle, 322), the first and second centuries of the Roman Empire, Italy in the fifteenth and early sixteenth centuries, and from the end of the Fronde, 1653, to the Revolution. For my part, I should be inclined to subtract from these the Roman period, and add, if only I knew more about it, the age of Sung. But accepting, by way of compromise, all five, we find that three—the Greek, Chinese, and Italian—were rich in visual art, whereas Rome was utterly barren and the eighteenth century not extraordinarily prolific. To make matters worse, we see in the dark and early middle ages a steady flow of first-rate art from societies more or less barbarous, while lately we have learnt that black and naked savages can create exquisitely.

Are we, then, to assume that there is no connection between art and civilization? I think not. A connection there is, but, as was to be expected, an unessential one. The essential quality in art is invariable, and what gives the Parthenon its significance is what gives significance to a nigger's basket-work box. There is such a thing as civilized art, but its civility lies in adventitious and subsidiary qualities—in the means, not in the end. It seems to me we do mean something when we say that Phidias, Sophocles, and Aristophanes, Raphael, Racine, Molière, Poussin, Milton, Wren, Jane Austen and Mozart are highly civilized artists, and that the creators of the Gothic cathedrals and the author of the *Chanson de Roland*, Villon, Webster, Rembrandt, Blake, Wordsworth, Emily Brontë, Whitman, Turner, Wagner and the Congolese fetish-makers are not. But, whatever we may mean, assuredly we do not mean that one set is superior to the other. They differ widely; but they differ in the means by which they compass the same end. It is absurd to argue that civilization is either favourable or unfavourable to art; but it is reasonable to suppose that it may be the one or the other to a particular artist. Different temperaments thrive in different atmospheres. How many mute, inglorious Miltons, Raphaels, and Mozarts may not have lost heart and gone under in the savage insecurity of the dark ages ? And may not the eighteenth century, which clipped the wings of Blake, have crushed the fluttering aspirations of a dozen Gothically-minded geniuses and laughed some budding Wagner out of all idea of expressing his ebullient personality ?

It is possible to speak of civilized or un-civilized art and mean something by our words ; but what we mean has nothing to do with the ultimate value of the work. And, in the same way, there may be an unessential connection between art and politics, though more remote and unimportant still. As I have explained too often already, an artist, before he can create effectively, has got to work himself into a passion ; by some means he has got to raise his feelings to the creative temperature and his energies to a corresponding pitch of intensity. He must make himself drunk somehow, and political passion is as good a tipple as another. Religion, Science, Morals, Love, Hate, Fear, Lust—all serve the artist's turn, and Politics and Patriotism have done their bit. It is clear that Wordsworth was thrown into the

state of mind in which he wrote his famous
sonnets by love of England and detestation of
France, by fear of revolution and longing for
order ; but how much patriotism or constitu-
tionalism has to do with the suave beauty of
those harmonious masterpieces may be inferred
from the fact that " hoarse FitzGerald " and
Mr. Kipling are quite as patriotic and even
more reactionary. Amongst painters David
is the conspicuous example of an artist—a small
one, to be sure—intoxicated by politics. David
set out as a humble, eighteenth-century follower
of Fragonard. But the Revolution filled his
poor head with notions about the Greeks and
the Romans, Harmodius and Aristogiton,
Cornelia and the Gracchi, *sic semper tyrannis*,
and Phrygian caps. And his revolutionary enthusiasm changed the whole manner of his
attack on that central, artistic problem which
never, in any style, did he succeed in solving.
But the influence of this new style was immense,
and paramount in French painting for the next
forty or fifty years. It is to be noted, however,
that David's great and immediate follower, the
mighty Ingres, who frankly adopted this style,
redolent of all republican virtues, was himself
one of the most virulent reactionaries that ever
lived.

And that, perhaps, would be all that needed
saying about Art and Politics were it not that
at this moment the subject has an unusual im-

portance. Movements in art have, more often than not, been the result of an extraordinarily violent preoccupation, on the part of artists, with the unessential and insignificant. David rescued painting from the charming and slightly sentimental disorder of the later eighteenth century by concentrating on Roman virtues and generals' uniforms. The Romantics freed themselves from Davidism by getting frantically excited about a little hazy nonsense rather unfairly attributed to Lord Byron and Sir Walter Scott. From this the Impressionists escaped by persuading themselves that they were men of science. And against this my contemporaries set up a conscious æstheticism, slightly tinged with certain metaphysico-moral doctrines concerning the cowiness of cows and the thing in itself. With Cubism conscious æstheticism holds the field, for the Cubist theory is, in the main, æsthetic. That is one reason why I cannot think that there is any great future for Cubism. An artistic movement is unlikely to live long on anything so relevant to art ; for artists, it seems, must believe that they are concerned with something altogether different. Wherefore, I think it not improbable—indeed, there are indications already *—that, political progress having in the last few years somewhat outrun civilization, and the new democracy being apparently hos-

* September 1920

tile to art and culture, artists will take to believing passionately in what they will call " order." If so, in the name of Napoleon and Louis XIV, but, let us hope, with the science and restraint of Poussin and Ingres, they will turn, most likely, to the classical tradition and, while endeavouring to create significant form, will assert vehemently that they are expressing their political convictions.

THE AUTHORITY OF
M. DERAIN

Sooner or later the critic who wishes to be taken seriously must say his word about Derain. It is an alarming enterprise. Not only does he run a considerable risk of making himself absurd, he may make a formidable and contemptuous enemy as well. " On ne peut pas me laisser tranquille ! " grumbles Derain ; to which the only reply I can think of is—" on ne peut pas."

Derain is now the greatest power amongst young French painters. I would like to lay stress on the words " power " and " French," because I do not wish to say, what may nevertheless be true, that Derain is the greatest painter in France, or seemingly to forget that Picasso's is the paramount influence in Europe. For all their abjurations most of the younger and more intelligent foreigners, within and without the gates of Paris, know well enough that Picasso is still their animator. Wherever a trace of Cubism or of *tête-de-nègre*, or of that thin, anxious line of the " blue period " is still to be found, there the ferment of his unquiet spirit is at work. And I believe it is in revolt against, perhaps in terror of, this profoundly un-French spirit that the younger Frenchmen are seeking shelter and grace under the vast though unconscious nationalism of Derain.

For the French have never loved Cubism,

though Braque uses it beautifully. How should they love anything so uncongenial to their temperament ? How should that race which above all others understands and revels in life care for an art of abstractions ? How, having raised good sense to the power of genius, should France quite approve æsthetic fanaticism ? What would Poussin have said to so passionate a negation of common sense ? Well, happily, we know the opinion of Molière :

La parfaite raison fuit toute extrémité,
Et veut que l'on soit sage avec sobriété.

Did ever Frenchmen sympathize absolutely with Don Quixote ? At any rate, because at the very base of his civilization lies that marvellous sense of social relations and human solidarity, a French artist will never feel entirely satisfied unless he can believe that his art is somehow related to, and justified by, Life.

Now, Picasso is not Spanish for nothing. He is a mystic ; which, of course, does not prevent him being a remarkably gay and competent man of the world. Amateurs who knew him in old days are sometimes surprised to find Picasso now in a comfortable flat or staying at the Savoy. I should not be surprised to hear of him in a Kaffir kraal or at Buckingham Palace, and wherever he might be I should know that under that urbane and slightly quizzical surface still would be kicking and struggling the tireless problem. That problem his circumstances cannot touch. It has nothing to do with Life; for not only was Picasso never satisfied with a line that did not seem right in the eyes of God—of the God that is in him, I mean—but never would it occur to him that a line could be right in any other way. For him Life proves nothing and signifies not much; it is the raw material of art. His problem is within; for ever he is straining and compelling his instrument to sing in unison with that pitiless voice which in El Greco's day they called the voice of God. Derain's problem is different, and perhaps more exacting still.

It seems odd, I know, but I think it is true to say that Derain's influence over the younger Frenchmen depends as much on his personality as on his pictures. Partly this may be because his pictures are not much to be seen; for he is neither prolific not particularly diligent, and always there are half a dozen hungry dealers waiting to snap up whatever he may contrive to finish. But clearly this is not explanation enough, and to appreciate Derain's position in Paris one should be, what unluckily I am not, a psychologist. One should be able to understand why his pictures are imitated hardly at all, and why his good opinion is coveted; why young painters want to know what Derain thinks and feels, not only about their art, but about art in general, and even about life; and why instinctively they pay him this compliment of supposing that he does not wish them simply to paint as he paints. What is it Derain wants of them? I shall be satisfied, and a good deal surprised, if I can discover even what he wants of himself.

A year or two ago it was the fashion to insist on Derain's descent from the Italian Primitives: I insisted with the rest. But as he matures his French blood asserts more and more its sovranty, and now completely dominates the other elements in his art. Assuredly he is in the great European tradition, but specifically he is of the French: Chardin, Watteau, and Poussin are his direct ancestors. Of Poussin no one who saw *La Boutique Fantasque* will have forgotten how it made one think. No one will have forgotten the grave beauty of those sober greys, greens, browns, and blues. They made one think of Poussin, and of Racine, too. And yet the ballet was intensely modern; always you were aware that Derain had been right through the movement—through Fauvism, Negroism, Cubism. Here was an artist who had refused nothing and feared nothing. Could anyone be less of a reactionary and at the same time less of an anarchist? And, I will add, could anyone be less *gavroche*? *La Boutique Fantasque*, which is not only the most amusing, but the most beautiful, of Russian ballets, balances on a discord. Even the fun of Derain is not the essentially modern fun of Massine. Derain is neither flippant nor exasperated; he is humorous, and tragic sometimes.

English criticizm is puzzled by Derain because very often it is confronted by things of his which seem dull and commonplace, to English critics. These are, in fact, the protests of Derain's genius against his talent, and whether they are good or not I cannot say. Derain has a super-natural gift for making things : give him a tin kettle and in half a morning he will hammer you out a Summerian head ; he has the fingers of a pianist, an aptitude that brings beauty to life with a turn of the wrist ; in a word, that sensibility of touch which keeps an ordinary craftsman happy for a lifetime : and these things terrify him. He ties both hands behind his back and fights so. Deliberately he chooses the most commonplace aspects and the most unlovely means of expression, hoping that, talent thus bound, genius will be stung into action. Sometimes, no doubt, Achilles stays sulking in his tent. I suppose Derain can be dull.

But what does he want this genius of his to do ? Nothing less, I believe, than what the French genius did at its supreme moment, in the seventeenth century, what the Greek did in the fifth. My notion is that he wants to create art which shall be perfectly uncompromising and at the same time human, and he would like it none the worse, I dare say, were it to turn out popular as well. After all, Racine did this, and Molière and La Bruyère and Watteau and Chardin and Renoir. It is in the French tradition to believe that there is a beauty common to life and art. The Greeks had it, so runs the argument, and the Italians of the high renaissance, but the English poets tended to sacrifice art to beauty, and the moderns—so Derain may think—sacrifice beauty and grandeur to discretion. The motto "Safety first" did, I will confess, just float across my eyes as I walked through the last *salon d'automne*. And, then, Derain may feel that there is in him something besides his power of creation and sense of form, something which philosophers would call, I dare say, a sense of absolute beauty in things, of external harmony. However we may call it, what I mean is the one thing at all worth having which the Greeks had and the Byzantines had not, which Raphael possesses more abundantly than Giotto. In Derain this sense is alive and insistent; it is urging him always to capture something that is outside him; the question is, can he, without for one moment compromising the purity of his art, obey it? I do not know. But if he cannot, then there is no man alive to give this age what Phidias, Giorgione, and Watteau gave theirs.

THE AUTHORITY OF M. DERAIN

The French are not unwilling to believe that they are the heirs of Greece and Rome. So, if I am right, the extraordinary influence of Derain may be accounted for partly, at any rate, by the fact that he, above all living Frenchmen, has the art to mould, in the materials of his age, a vessel that might contain the grand classical tradition. What is more, it is he, if anyone, who has the strength to fill it. No one who ever met him but was impressed by the prodigious force of his character and his capacity for standing alone. At moments he reminds one oddly of Johnson. He, too, is a dictator, at once humorous and tragic like the mirific doctor, but, unlike him, infinitely subtle. He, too, is troubled, and not by any sense of isolation nor yet by the gnawings of vanity and small ambition. It is the problem that tortures him. Can he do what Raphael and Racine did ? Can he create something that shall be uncompromising as art and at the same time humane ?

Face to face with that problem Derain stands for what is to-day most vital and valid in France —a passionate love of the great tradition, a longing for order and the will to win it, and that mysterious thing which the Athenians called σπουδαιότης and schoolmasters call " high seriousness." He accepts the age into which he has stumbled with all its nastiness, vulgarity, and cheek. He accepts that woebegone, modern democracy which could not even make its great war fine. He believes he can make something of it. Because he has a first-rate intellect he can afford to mistrust reason ; and so sure is he of his own taste that he can brush refinement aside. Yet neither his scepticisms nor his superstitions alienate the intelligent, nor are the sensitive offended by his total disregard of their distinctions. And though all this has nothing to do with painting, on painters, I surmise, it has its effect.

"PLUS DE JAZZ"*

On the first night of the Russian ballet in Paris, somewhere about the middle of May, perhaps the best painter in France, one of the best musicians, and an obscure journalist were sitting in a small *bistrot* on the Boulevard St. Germain. They should all have been at the spectacle; all had promised to go; and yet they sat on over their *alcools* and *bocks*, and instead of going to the ballet began to abuse it. And from the ballet they passed to modern music in general, and from music to literature : till gradually into the conversation came, above the familiar note of easy denigration, a note of energy, of conviction, of aspiration, which so greatly astonished one, at least, of the three that, just before two o'clock—the hour at which the patron puts even his most faithful clients out of doors—he exclaimed, with an emphasis in him uncommon, " Plus de Jazz ! "

It was the least important of the three who said it, and, had it been the most, I am not suggesting that, like the walls of Jericho, a movement would have tottered at an ejaculation. Jazz will not die because a few clever people have discovered that they are getting sick of it ; Jazz is dying, and the conversation to which I have referred is of importance only as an early recognition of the fact. For the rest it was unjust, as such conversations will be ;

* 1921

213

the Jazz movement, short and slightly irritating
though it was, having served its turn and added
its quota to the tradition. But Jazz is dead—
or dying, at any rate—and the moment has
come for someone who likes to fancy himself
wider awake than his fellows to write its
obituary notice. In doing so he may, adventitiously, throw light on something more
interesting than the past ; he may adumbrate
the outline of the coming movement. For
always movements are conditioned partly by
their predecessors, against which, in some sort,
they must ever be reactions.

The Jazz movement is a ripple on a wave ;
the wave—the large movement which began at
the end of the nineteenth century in a reaction
against realism and scientific paganism—still
goes forward. The wave is essentially the movement which one tends to associate, not very
accurately perhaps, with the name of Cézanne :
it has nothing to do with Jazz ; its most
characteristic manifestation is modern painting,
which, be it noted, Jazz had left almost untouched. " Picasso ? " queries someone. I shall
come to Picasso presently. The great modern
painters—Derain, Matisse, Picasso, Bonnard,
Friesz, Braque, etc.—were firmly settled on their
own lines of development before ever Jazz was
heard of : only the riff-raff has been affected.
Italian Futurism is the nearest approach to a
pictorial expression of the Jazz spirit.

" PLUS DE JAZZ "

The movement bounced into the world somewhere about the year 1911. It was headed by
a Jazz band and a troupe of niggers, dancing.
Appropriately it took its name from music—
the art that is always behind the times. Gavroche was killed on the barricades, and it was
with his name that Jazz should have been
associated. Impudence is its essence—impudence in quite natural and legitimate revolt
against nobility and beauty : impudence which
finds its technical equivalent in syncopation :
impudence which rags. " The Ragtime movement " would have been the better style, but
the word " Jazz " has passed into at least
three languages, and now we must make the
best of it.

After impudence comes the determination
to surprise: you shall not be gradually moved
to the depths, you shall be given such a start
as makes you jigger all over. And from this
determination issues the grateful corollary—
thou shalt not be tedious. The best Jazz
artists are never long-winded. In their admirable and urbane brevity they remind one
rather of the French eighteenth century. But
surprise is an essential ingredient. An accomplished Jazz artist, whether in notes or words,
will contrive, as a rule, to stop just where
you expected him to begin. Themes and
ideas are not to be developed ; to say all one
has to say smells of the school, and may be

a bore, and—between you and me—a "give-away" to boot. Lastly, it must be admitted there is a typically modern craving for small profits and quick returns. Jazz art is soon created, soon liked, and soon forgotten. It is the movement of masters of eighteen; and these masterpieces created by boys barely escaped from college can be appreciated by the youngest Argentine beauty at the Ritz. Jazz is very young: like short skirts, it suits thin, girlish legs, but has a slightly humiliating effect on grey hairs. Its fears and dislikes—for instance, its horror of the noble and the beautiful—are childish; and so is its way of expressing them. Not by irony and sarcasm, but by jeers and grimaces does Jazz mark its antipathies. Irony and wit are for the grown-ups. Jazz dislikes them as much as it dislikes nobility and beauty. They are the products of the cultivated intellect, and Jazz cannot away with intellect or culture. Niggers can be admired artists without any gifts more singular than high spirits; so why drag in the intellect? Besides, to bring intellect into art is to invite home a guest who is apt to be inquisitive and even impartial. Intellect in Jazz circles is treated rather as money was once in polite society—it is taken for granted. Nobility, beauty, and intellectual subtlety are alike ruled out: the first two are held up to ridicule, the last is simply abused. What Jazz wants are romps and fun, and to make fun ; that is why, as I have said, its original name Ragtime was the better. At its best Jazz rags every thing.

The inspiration of Jazz is the same as that of the art of the *grand siècle*. Everyone knows how in the age of Louis XIV artists found in *la bonne compagnie* their standards, their critics, and many of their ideas. It was by studying and writing for this world that Racine, Molière, and Boileau gave an easier and less professional gait to French literature, which—we should not forget—during its most glorious period was conditioned and severely limited by the tastes and prejudices of polite society. Whether the inventors of Jazz thought that, in their pursuit of beauty and intensity, the artists of the nineteenth century had strayed too far from the tastes and interests of common but well-to-do humanity I know not, but certain it is that, like Racine and Molière, and unlike Beaudelaire and Mallarmé and César Franck, they went to *la bonne compagnie* for inspiration and support. *La bonne compagnie* they found in the lounges of great hotels, on transatlantic liners, in *wagons-lits*, in music-halls, and in expensive motor-cars and restaurants. *La bonne compagnie* was dancing one-steps to ragtime music. This, they said, is the thing. The artists of the nineteenth century had found *la bonne compagnie*—the rich, that is to say— dancing waltzes to sentimental *Olgas* and

Blue Danubes, but they had drawn quite other conclusions. Yet waltzes and waltz-tunes are just as good as, and no better than, fox-trots and ragtime. Both have their merits ; but it is a mistake, perhaps, for artists to take either seriously.

Be that as it may, the serious artists of the nineteenth century never dreamed of supposing that the pleasures of the rich were the proper stuff of art ; so it was only natural that the twentieth should go to the hotel lounges for inspiration. And, of course, it was delightful for those who sat drinking their cocktails and listening to nigger-bands to be told that, besides being the jolliest people on earth, they were the most sensitive and critically gifted. They, along with the children and savages whom in so many ways they resembled, were the possessors of natural, uncorrupted taste. They first had appreciated ragtime and surrendered themselves to the compelling qualities of Jazz. Their instinct might be trusted : so, no more classical concerts and music-lessons ; no more getting Lycidas by heart ; no more Bædeker ; no more cricking one's neck in the Sistine Chapel : unless the coloured gentleman who leads the band at the Savoy has a natural leaning towards these things you may depend upon it they are noble, pompous, and fraudulent. And it was delightful, too, for people without a vestige of talent—and even then these were in the majority—people who could just strum a tune or string a few lines of doggerel, to be told that all that distinguishes what used to be called " serious art " from their productions was of no consequence whatever, and that, on the contrary, it was these, if any, that ought to be taken seriously. The output of verse, which was manifestly much too easy to write and difficult to read, went up suddenly by leaps and bounds. What is more, some of it got printed : publishers, and even editors, bowed the knee. Naturally, the movement was a success at the Ritz and in Grub Street, Mayfair. On the other hand, because to people who reflected for an instant it seemed highly improbable that fox-trotters and shimmy-shakers were sensitive or interesting people, that Christy Minstrels were great musicians, or that pub-crawlers and *demi-mondaines* were poets, there sprang simultaneously into existence a respectable, intelligent, and ill-tempered opposition which did, and continues to do, gross injustice to the genuine artists who have drawn inspiration, or sustenance at any rate, from Jazz.

During the last ten years Jazz had dominated music and coloured literature : on painting, as I have said, its effect has been negligible. What, for want of a better name, I must call the Cézanne movement was too profound a stream to be modified by so shallow a current.

All the great contemporary painters are extremely serious ; they make no faces at their predecessors, or at anyone else. They are not *gavroche*. Surprise is the last emotion they wish to arouse. And, assuredly, they have neither gone to the hotel-loungers for inspiration nor shown the slightest desire to amuse them. This is as true of Picasso as of Derain : only, Picasso's prodigious inventiveness may sometimes give the impression of a will to surprise, while his habit of turning everything to account certainly does lead him to cast an inquisitive eye on every new manifestation of vitality. I have seen him enthusiastic over *la politique* Lloyd-George, and I should not be in the least surprised if he found something in it to serve some one or other of his multifarious purposes. If, however, surprise were what Picasso aimed at he could go a very much easier way about it. He could do what his tenth-rate imitators try to do—for instance, he could agreeably shock the public with monstrous caricatures and cubist photography—those pictures, I mean, which the honest stockbroker recognizes, with a thrill of excitement at his own cleverness, as his favourite picture-postcards rigged out to look naughty. But Picasso shows such admirable indifference to the public that you could never guess from his pictures that such a thing existed : and that, of course, is how it should be. He never startles for the sake of

startling ; neither does he mock. Certainly,
unlike the best of his contemporaries, he seems
almost as indifferent to the tradition as he
is to the public ; but he no more laughs at the
one than he tries to startle the other. Only
amongst the whipper-snappers of painting will
you discover a will to affront tradition, or attract attention by deliberate eccentricity. Only,
I think, the Italian Futurists, their transalpine
apes, a few revolutionaries on principle, but
especially the Futurists with their electric-lit
presentation of the more obvious peculiarities
of contemporary life and their taste for popular
actualities can be said definitely to have attempted a pictorial expression of Jazz.

On music, however, and literature its influence has been great, and here its triumphs
are considerable. It is easy to say that the
genius of Stravinsky—a musician, unless I
mistake, of the first order and in the great line
—rises superior to movements. To be sure
it does : so does the genius of Molière. But
just as the genius of Molière found its appropriate food in one kind of civilization, so does
the genius of Stravinsky in another ; and with
that civilization his art must inevitably be
associated. Technically, too, he has been influenced much by nigger rhythms and nigger
methods. He has composed ragtimes. So,
if it is inexact to say that Stravinsky writes Jazz,
it is true to say that his genius has been

nourished by it. Also, he sounds a note of defiance, and sometimes, I think, does evince a will to insult. That he surprises and startles is clear ; what is more, 1 believe he means to do it : but tricks of self-advertisement are, of course, beneath so genuine an artist. No more than Picasso does he seek small profits or quick returns ; on the contrary, he casts his bread upon the waters with a finely reckless gesture. The fact is, Stravinsky is too big to be covered by a label ; but I think the Jazz movement has as much right to claim him for its own as any movement has to claim any first-rate artist. Similarly, it may claim Mr. T. S. Eliot—a poet of uncommon merit and unmistakably in the great line—whose agonizing labours seem to have been eased somewhat by the comfortable ministrations of a black and grinning muse Midwifery, to be sure, seems an odd occupation for a lady whom one pictures rather in the rôle of a flapper : but a midwife was what the poet needed, and in that capacity she has served him. Apparently it is only by adopting a demurely irreverent attitude, by being primly insolent, and by playing the devil with the instrument of Shakespeare and Milton that Mr. Eliot is able occasionally to deliver himself of one of those complicated and remarkable imaginings of his : apparently it is only in language of an exquisite purity so far as material goes, but twisted and ragged out of

easy recognition, that these nurslings can be
swathed. As for surprise, that, presumably,
is an emotion which the author of *Ara Vos Prec*
is not unwilling to provoke. Be that as it may,
Mr. Eliot is about the best of our living poets,
and, like Stravinsky, he is as much a product of
the Jazz movement as so good an artist can be
of any.

In literature Jazz manifests itself both
formally and in content. Formally its distinc-
tive characteristic is the familiar one—syncopation. It has given us a ragtime literature
which flouts traditional rhythms and sequences
and grammar and logic. In verse its products
—rhythms which are often indistinguishable
from prose rhythms and collocations of words
to which sometimes is assignable no exact
intellectual significance—are by now familiar
to all who read. Eliot is too personal to be
typical of anything, and the student who would
get a fair idea of Jazz poetry would do better
to spend half an hour with a volume of Cocteau
or Cendrars. In prose I think Mr. Joyce will
serve as a, perhaps, not very good example :
I choose him because he is probably better
known to readers than any other writer who
affects similar methods. In his later publications Mr. Joyce does deliberately go to work
to break up the traditional sentence, throwing
overboard sequence, syntax, and, indeed, most
of those conventions which men habitually

employ for the exchange of precise ideas. Effectually, and with a will, he rags the literary instrument: unluckily, this will has at its service talents which though genuine are moderate only. A writer of greater gifts, Virginia Woolf, has lately developed a taste for playing tricks with traditional constructions. Certainly she " leaves out " with the boldest of them : here is syncopation if you like it. I am not sure that I do. At least, I doubt whether the concentration gained by her new style for *An Unwritten Novel* and *Monday or Tuesday* makes up for the loss of those exquisite but old-fashioned qualities which make *The Mark on the Wall* a masterpiece of English prose. But, indeed, I do not think of Mrs. Woolf as belonging properly to the movement ; she is not imbued with that spirit which inspires the authentic Jazz writers, whether of verse that looks oddly like prose or of prose that raises a false hope of turning out to be verse, and conditions all that they produce. She is not *gavroche*. In her writings I find no implicit, and often well-merited, jeer at accepted ideas of what prose and verse should be and what they should be about ; no nervous dislike of traditional valuations, of scholarship, culture, and intellectualism ; above all, no note of protest against the notion that one idea or emotion can be more important or significant than another. Assuredly, Mrs. Woolf is not of the company on whose banner

is inscribed " No discrimination ! " " No culture ! " " Not much thought ! " She is not
of that school whose grand object it is to present, as surprisingly as possible, the chaos of
any mind at any given moment.

The Jazz theory of art, if theory there be,
seems stupid enough—as do most. What
matters, however, are not theories, but works :
so what of the works of Jazz ? If Stravinsky
is to be claimed for the movement, Jazz has its
master : it has also its *petits maîtres*—Eliot,
Cendrars, Picabia, and Joyce, for instance, and
les six. Oddly enough, *les six* consist of four
musicians—Darius Milhaud, Georges Auric,
Poulenc, and Germaine Taillefer*—chaperoned
by the brilliant Jean Cocteau. All five have
their places in contemporary civilization : and
such talents are not to be disposed of simply by
the present of a bad name. For it is not enough
to call an artist " extremist " or " reactionary,"
"Cubist" or " Impressionist," and condemn
or approve him as such. These classifications
are merely journalistic or, if you will, archæological conveniences. It is the critic's business
to inquire not so much whether an artist is
" advanced " or " Cubist " or " Jazz," as
whether he is good, bad, or interesting ; and
that is what most critics fail to do. One's
general opinion of a movement or school ought
not to affect one's opinion of any particular

* Honegger, I think, was never officially of the band.

work. One may, for excellent reasons, dislike a movement ; one may hold that it hampers
or sets on a false scent more artists than it
serves ; that it induces students of promise to
waste time and energy on fruitless problems ;
that it generally fails to get the best out of its
most gifted adherents, while it pumps into a
multitude of empty heads so much hot air as to
swell them to disquieting proportions. This is
pretty much what I think of Cubism ; but I
am not such a fool as to deny that, experiment-
ing in these very problems which seem to me
to lead most artists into a rather unprofitable
world of abstractions, Picasso and Braque have
produced works of the greatest beauty and
significance, while those of Fernand Léger,
Jean Metsinger, and other avowed Cubists are
of extraordinary merit and deserve the most
careful attention. I can think of no movement except that called "Art nouveau," which
has not contributed something to the world's
artistic capital and to the great tradition. Only,
to realize this, one must be able to distinguish
not only between movements, but between the
artists of a movement. That is what angry
critics will not do. That is why the admirable
Mr. Dent—whose brilliant lacerations of *les six*,
and other exponents of Jazz, I sometimes have
the pleasure of translating to his victims—knew
no better, the other day, than to bracket
Poulenc with Miss Edith Sitwell. Confusions

of this sort seem to me to take the sting out of
criticism ; and that, I am sure, is the last thing
Mr. Dent would wish to do. He, at any rate,
who comes to bury Jazz should realize what
the movement has to its credit, *viz.*, one great
musician, one considerable poet, ten or a dozen
charming or interesting little masters and
mistresses, and a swarm of utterly fatuous
creatures who in all good faith believe themselves artists.

The encouragement given to fatuous ignorance to swell with admiration of its own in-
competence is perhaps what has turned most
violently so many intelligent and sensitive
people against Jazz. They see that it en-
courages thousands of the stupid and vulgar
to fancy that they can understand art, and
hundreds of the conceited to imagine that they
can create it. All the girls in the " dancings "
and sportsmen at the bar who like a fox-trot or
a maxixe have been given to believe, by people
who ought to know better, that they are more
sensitive to music than those who prefer
Beethoven. The fact that Stravinsky wants
his music to be enjoyed in the cafés gives pub-
loafers fair ground for supposing that Stravinsky respects their judgement. Well, the
music of Brahms is not enjoyed by pub-loafers ;
but formerly the concert-goers were allowed
to know better. Stravinsky is reported to have
said that he would like people to be eating,

drinking, and talking while his music was being played (how furious he would be if they did anything of the sort!), so, when a boxful of bounders begin chattering in the middle of an opera and the cultivated cry " hush " the inference is that the cultivated are making themselves ridiculous. Again : if rules were made by pedants for pedants, must not mere lawlessness be a virtue ? And, since savages think little and know less, and since savage art has been extolled by the knowing ones (I take my share of whatever blame may be going) as much as " cultured " has been decried does it not follow that ignorant and high-spirited lads are likely to write better verses than such erudite old buffers as Milton, Spenser, and Gray ? Above all, because it has been said that the intellect has nothing to do with art, it is assumed by the mob of ladies and gentlemen, who if they wrote not with ease could not write at all, that there is no such thing as the artistic problem. And it is, I believe, chiefly because all genuine artists are beginning to feel more and more acutely the need of a severe and exacting problem, and because everyone who cares seriously for art feels the need of severe critical standards, that, with a sigh of relief, people are timidly murmuring to each other " Plus de Jazz ! "

And, indeed, there are autumnal indications : the gay *papier-mâché* pagoda is beginning to lose its colours : visibly it is wilting. When, a few days after the conversation I have recorded, it was rumoured in Paris that the admired Prokofieff, composer of *Chout*, had said that he detested ragtime, the consternation into which were thrown some fashionable bars and *salons* was as painful to behold as must have been that into which were thrown parlours and vicarage gardens when Professor Huxley began pouring cold water on Noah's Ark. We hurried away to the Southern Syncopated Orchestra, only to find it sadly fallen off. But had it really changed so much as we ? And, more and more, immense musical and literary activity notwithstanding, people are looking to the painters, with their high seriousness, professionalism, conscience, reverence, and vitality as the sole exponents and saviours of " le grand art." Not for nothing is Derain the most admired of Frenchmen by the young *élite* ; for Derain is humorous without being *gavroche*, respects the tradition yet is subservient to no school, and believes that all the highest human faculties are not more than sufficient to the production of the smallest work of art.

What the pick of the new generation in France, and in England too, I fancy, is beginning to feel is that art, though it need never be solemn, must always be serious ; that it is a matter of profound emotion and of intense

and passionate thought; and that these things
are rarely found in dancing-palaces and hotel
lounges. Even to understand art a man must
make a great intellectual effort. One thing is
not as good as another; so artists and amateurs
must learn to choose. No easy matter that:
discrimination of this sort being something
altogether different from telling a Manhattan
from a Martini. To select as an artist or discriminate as a critic are needed feeling and
intellect and—most distressing of all—study.
However, unless I mistake, the effort will be
made. The age of easy acceptance of the
first thing that comes is closing. Thought
rather than spirits is required, quality rather
than colour, knowledge rather than irreticence,
intellect rather than singularity, wit rather than
romps, precision rather than surprise, dignity
rather than impudence, and lucidity above all
things : *plus de Jazz*. Meanwhile, whether
the ladies and gentlemen in the restaurants will
soon be preferring sentimental waltz-tunes to
flippant ragtimes is a question on which I cannot pretend to an opinion. Neither does it
matter. What these people like or dislike has
nothing to do with art. That is the discovery.

Printed in Great Britain
by T. and A. Constable Ltd.
at the University Press
Edinburgh

THE PHOENIX LIBRARY

IT has been the aim of Messrs. Chatto & Windus in this series, which will mainly consist of reprints, to design a book which will be suitable alike for the pocket and the shelf, as travelling companion and as household friend. The volumes are printed on choice paper and are of equal bulk, about half an inch; in surface they measure $4\frac{1}{2}$ inches by 7. They are stoutly bound, and are characterized by this innovation, that the works of particular authors are all bound in one colour. Thus the works of Mr. Lytton Strachey appear in a uniform shade of green, and it would therefore be possible to group together on the shelf *Queen Victoria*, *Eminent Victorians*, and *Books and Characters* apart from the other books in the same series; and so on.

UNIFORM PRICE, 3s. 6d. net.

NUMBER
1. QUEEN VICTORIA *by* Lytton Strachey.

This book is well-known as the greatest acievement of modern biography in the English language. It was awarded the James Tait Black Memorial Prize for 1922.

2. EMINENT VICTORIANS
by Lytton Strachey.

Studies of Cardinal Manning, Florence Nightingale, Dr. Arnold of Rugby and General Gordon. The book that first made Mr. Strachey famous.

3. ANTIC HAY *by* ALDOUS HUXLEY.
A novel. 'Mr. Huxley's delicate sureness with words gives an air of indestructibility to this book.' *The Evening Standard*.

4. ALONG THE ROAD *by* ALDOUS HUXLEY.
Further described by the sub-title: 'Notes and Essays of a Tourist.' One of Mr. Huxley's most delightful collections of essays, subdivided into 'Travel in General,' 'Places,' 'Works of Art,' and 'By the Way.'

5. TALES OF THE FIVE TOWNS
by ARNOLD BENNETT.
Mr. Bennet's material is here his very own; the principal characters come from the Staffordshire Potteries, the part of England which has given Mr. Bennett inspiration for his best books.

6. THE MERCY OF ALLAH
by HILAIRE BELLOC.
A series of tales about a rascally merchant of Baghdad and the different ways in which he made his money; Mr. Belloc's masterpiece in the satirical-picaresque.

7. LADY INTO FOX and A MAN IN THE
ZOO *by* DAVID GARNETT.
Lady into Fox was a new literary creation. It was awarded the Hawthornden and the James Tait Black Memorial Prizes for 1923. The composite volume is illustrated with all the original woodcuts by R. A. Garnett.

8. BOOKS & CHARACTERS
by LYTTON STRACHEY.
These studies are mainly of literary subjects, as Racine, Sir Thomas Browne, Voltaire, Blake and Stendhal. In reviewing this book, *The Times* said: 'Mr. Strachey's is perhaps the finest critical intelligence at work in English literature to-day.'

9. FIERY PARTICLES *by* C. E. MONTAGUE.
'Nine of the best short stories in the language,' was the verdict of *The Sunday Express;* ' . . better than Kipling.'

10. FIRST PLAYS *by* A. A. MILNE.

This volume contains 'Wurzel-Flummery,' 'The Lucky One,' 'The Boy Comes Home,' 'Belinda,' and 'The Red Feathers.'

11. CROME YELLOW *by* ALDOUS HUXLEY.

Mr. Huxley's first novel, perhaps his gayest. On its appearance it was hailed by *The Spectator* as 'a delightful book.'

12. ART *by* CLIVE BELL.

In this book Mr. Clive Bell first propounded his theory of significant form. *Art* still remains the best short treatise in the English language on the æsthetics of visual art, as well as the best introduction to the study of the Post-Impressionist painters.

13. DISENCHANTMENT
by C. E. MONTAGUE.

Mr. Montague's famous diagnosis of the moral results of the War. 'I have seen no book about the War so temperate and so human.' *John Masefield* in *The Manchester Guardian*.

14. THOSE BARREN LEAVES
by ALDOUS HUXLEY.

A long novel. 'It is impossible to exhaust it at a first reading, and it should be kept and dipped into again and again.' *The Empire Review*.

15. VISION AND DESIGN *by* ROGER FRY.

Essays on art and artists by a master critic. Among the subjects are: Art and Life, The Artist's Vision, Negro Sculpture, The French Post-Impressionists, etc. 'It is a long time since we have come across a book so stimulating.' *The Daily Chronicle*.

16. ESSAYS OF A BIOLOGIST
by JULIAN HUXLEY.

By the Professor of Zoology at King's College, the University of London. 'A brilliant book of serious purpose, and with a happy style; and it is by a maker of new biological knowledge who is also a scholar and a poet.' *Prof. J. Arthur Thomson* in *The Observer*.

23. MR. WESTON'S GOOD WINE
by T. F. POWYS.

The first unlimited edition of Mr. Powys's longest and greatest story, of which *The Bookman* said that it was 'worthy at once to take its place among the great allegories of English literature.'

24. LOLLY WILLOWES
by SYLVIA TOWNSEND WARNER.

The witch-story hailed by *The Times Literary Supplement* as 'an object lesson in the proper way of bringing Satan into modern fiction.'

25. ON THE MARGIN *by* ALDOUS HUXLEY.

Notes and essays on such subjects as 'Centenaries,' 'The Subject-Matter of Poetry,' 'Bibliophily,' 'Nationality in Love,' 'Chaucer,' etc. 'One of the most interesting and provocative of the younger generation of English men of letters.' *The Daily Telegraph*.

26. THE GRIM SMILE OF THE FIVE TOWNS *by* ARNOLD BENNETT.

All who have read and enjoyed Mr. Bennett's stories of the Five Towns will be glad of a reprint of this book. Here, as in all his Five Town stories, Mr. Bennett's humour and buoyancy are unfailing.

27. TARR *by* WYNDHAM LEWIS.

Mr. Wyndham Lewis's novel, long out of print, is here completely revised. From reviews of the first edition: —'This admirable novel. . . . A book of great importance . . . because it will become a date in literature . . . because here we have the forerunner of the prose and probably of the manner that is to come.' *The New Witness*. 'A thunderbolt.' *The Weekly Dispatch*.

28. LITTLE MEXICAN *by* ALDOUS HUXLEY.

Short stories, containing : 'Uncle Spencer,' 'Little Mexican,' 'Hubert and Minnie,' 'Fard,' 'The Portrait,' and 'Young Archimedes.' 'The opulence of Mr. Huxley's talent speaks in every page.' *The Observer*.

29. LOVE & FREINDSHIP *by* JANE AUSTEN.

And other Early Works now first published, with an Introduction by G. K. CHESTERTON, who writes: 'A thing to laugh over again and again.'

30. THREE PLAYS *by* A. A. MILNE.

Containing 'The Great Broxopp,' 'The Dover Road,' 'The Truth about Blayds.'

31. THE HOUSE WITH THE ECHO
by T. F. POWYS.

'Connoisseurs of the short story should not miss this little book, for Mr. Powys has a rare mastery of the art.' *The Evening Standard.*

32. SWANN'S WAY, vol. 1, *by* MARCEL PROUST.

Translated by C. K. SCOTT MONCRIEFF. 'M. Proust is a genius; and Mr. Scott Moncrieff has treated him like one.' *The Nation.*

33. SWANN'S WAY, vol. 2, *by* MARCEL PROUST.

Translated by C. K. SCOTT MONCRIEFF. 'The translator ... faced a task of prodigious difficulty with extraordinary success. Until it was done, it was unbelievable that it could be done so well.' *The London Mercury.*

34. ESSAYS IN POPULAR SCIENCE
by JULIAN HUXLEY.

'One of the few scientific books that is popular and scientific without patronising the reader.' *The Cambridge Review.*

35. A SHORT HISTORY OF ENGLAND
by G. K. CHESTERTON.

'He is at once the most concise and fullest historian this country has yet found.' *The Observer.*

36. TWO OR THREE GRACES
by ALDOUS HUXLEY.

Four stories. 'It is a joy to read . . . I have no hesitation in saying that of the younger men writing to-day, Mr. Huxley is in a class of himself.' *Ralph Straus* in *The Bystander*.

37. HADRIAN VII by FR. ROLFE
('Baron Corvo.')

A fine novel which has been some time out of print. 'It sparkles with wit and gleams with satire; and the writer displays a really remarkable knowledge . . . of Roman Catholic proceedings at the headquarters of the faith.' *The Daily Graphic*.

38. THE GENTLE ART OF COOKERY
by MRS. C. F. LEYEL *and* MISS OLGA HARTLEY.

A really original cookery book which 'no properly instituted home should be without.' *The Morning Post*.

*

FURTHER VOLUMES ARE IN PREPARATION

*

ALL LISTS POST FREE FROM

Chatto & Windus
97 & 99 St. Martin's Lane, W.C.2

Telephone: Gerrard 0127, 0128   *Telegrams: Bookstore, London*